GOD AND RACE

A GUIDE FOR MOVING BEYOND BLACK FISTS AND WHITE KNUCKLES

STUDY GUIDE | FIVE SESSIONS

JOHN SIEBELING AND WAYNE FRANCIS

with Beth Graybill

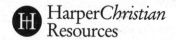

HarperChristian Resources

God and Race Study Guide
© 2021 by John Siebeling and Wayne Francis

Requests for information should be addressed to:
HarperChristian Resources, 3900 Sparks Dr. SE, Grand Rapids, Michigan 49546

ISBN 978-0-310-13794-8 (softcover)
ISBN 978-0-310-13795-5 (ebook)

HarperChristian Resources titles may be purchased in bulk for church, business, fundraising, or ministry use. For information, please e-mail ResourceSpecialist@ ChurchSource.com.

Published in association with The Fedd Agency, 401 Ranch Road 620 South, Suite 250, Austin, TX 78734.

First Printing September 2021 / Printed in the United States of America

CONTENTS

INTRODUCTION

At the end of the Bible, in the book of Revelation, we get an amazing glimpse of God's plan for race: "After this I looked, and there before me was a great multitude that no one could count, from every nation, tribe, people and language, standing before the throne and before the Lamb" (Revelation 7:9). The end of our story is a beautiful picture of a diverse group of people all worshiping together before God. This is where the church will end up one day.

But this is not necessarily how the church looks *today*. In fact, odds are that if you walk into a random church, it will look more like one single tribe, tongue, and nation. Multiracial churches are not certainly the norm. But we believe—with a lot of hard work and honest conversations—we can get there together. The change may not happen overnight, but if we all devote ourselves to discussions and commit to learning how to learn from one another through healthy dialogue, we can work together to build houses that look like heaven.

This is the purpose of the *God and Race* small-group study. Often, we in the church feel that the words *God* and *race* don't go together. They feel like unrelated topics. But nothing could be further from the truth! Diversity and unity are pivotal pieces of God's plan. For this reason, we want to give you a guide for understanding the issues of race and faith from both a *black* and *white* perspective. We also want to equip you with the tools you need to enter into open, honest, and fruitful conversations about God and race with confidence.

This study is meant to guide you and your fellow church members to move beyond *black fists* and *white knuckles*. We want to help you open your hands to the truth of the gospel and explore what it really has to say about race and how we interact with one another. We'll talk about allowing God to search our hearts to get us ready to engage in these conversations. We will then shift our focus externally and talk about your *household*—helping you to invite diversity into your home and your social circle. Finally, we'll talk about inviting diversity into the *house of God* and lay out some strategies for making that happen.

If you are brand new to the race conversation and scared to death that you are going to say the wrong thing . . . this study is for you.

If you are frustrated with the lack of attention your church is giving race relations and you're interested in being a part of the solution for positive change . . . this study is for you.

If you are a church leader unsure of how to take the next step to help your congregation get it . . . this study is for you.

If you are unsure what to believe about the current state of racial tension in our country . . . this study is for you.

If a friend handed you this book and you are only reading it to do them a favor . . . guess what? This study is for you.

The truth is, that as a nation, we are divided. We may not have created this division, but we are living in it. So, if you still have a pulse, you have a responsibility to be the answer and help push us forward toward the future God designed. Let this study be a guide along the way, because unless we make a solid and intentional choice to connect, understand, reach, and love one another, we will remain divided—and we can't afford to stay divided.

Let's loosen our grips, unclench our fists, open our hands, and come together.

— John Siebeling and Wayne Francis

HOW TO USE THIS GUIDE

The *God and Race* video study is designed to be experienced in a group setting (such as a Bible study, Sunday school class, or small-group gathering) and also as an individual study. Each session begins with a brief opening reflection and several icebreaker-type questions to get you and your group thinking about the topic. You will then watch a video with John Siebeling and Wayne Francis, which can be accessed via the streaming code found on the inside front cover. If you are doing the study with a group, you will then engage in some directed discussion and close each session with a time of personal reflection and prayer.

Each person should have his or her own study guide, which includes video teaching notes, group discussion questions, and between-sessions personal studies to help you reflect on and apply the material to your life during the week. You are also encouraged to have a copy of the *God and Race* book, as reading it alongside the curriculum will provide you with deeper insights and make the journey more meaningful. (See the "For Next Week" section for the chapters in the book that correspond to the material that your group is discussing.)

To get the most out of your group experience, keep the following points in mind. First, the real growth in this study will happen during your small-group time. This is where you will process the content of John's and Wayne's message, ask questions, and learn from others as you hear what God is doing in their lives. For this reason, it is important for you to be fully committed to the group and attend each session so that you can build trust and rapport with the other members. If you choose to only "go through the motions," or if you refrain from participating, there is a lesser chance you will find what you're looking for during this study.

Second, remember the goal of your small group is to serve as a place where people can share, learn about God, and build intimacy and friendship. For this reason, seek to make your group a "safe place." This means being honest about your thoughts and feelings and listening carefully to everyone else's opinion.

Third, resist the temptation to "fix" someone's problem or correct his or her theology, as that's not the purpose of your small-group time. Also, keep everything your group shares confidential. This will foster a rewarding sense of community in your group and create a place where people can heal, be challenged, and grow spiritually.

In between your group times, you can maximize the impact of the course by checking out the personal study guide activity. This individual study will help you personally reflect and actively respond to the lesson. For each session, you may wish to complete the personal study in one sitting or spread it over a few days (for example, working on it a half-hour per day on four different days that week). Note that if you are unable to finish (or even start!) your between-sessions personal study, you should attend the group study video session regardless. You are still wanted and welcome at the group even if you don't have your "homework" done.

Keep in mind this study is an opportunity for you to train in a new way of seeing the intersection of faith and race. The videos, discussions, and activities are simply meant to kick-start your imagination so that you are open not only to what God wants you to hear but also to how to apply that message to your life.

Sound good? Then let's get started!

OPEN YOUR HANDS

Perfect love drives out fear.

1 JOHN 4:18

Welcome

The most common question we hear about the conversation between black and white communities of faith is *how do we move forward from here?* The desire to move beyond racism—defined in our book as *prejudice plus power*—is real, and so is the lack of understanding about the best place to start in the conversation. A powerful place to start the conversation about race is by understanding two key symbols.

Symbolism is where we find the significance of *black fists* and *white knuckles.* The *black fist* is a symbol made famous at the 1968 Olympics when two African-American athletes, Tommie Smith and John Carlos, raised their fists during the medal ceremony as the Star-Spangled Banner played, symbolizing solidarity with the black community. Ever since, the *black fist* has become a symbol of standing up against the residue of segregation, slavery, and the systemic oppression that was, and still is, happening against black people in our country.

White knuckles are symbolic in this study of white Americans who are gripping to a long-standing paradigm of privilege that holds an advantage over people of color. When people try to hold on to the past, it is because something is *actually* slipping away—and they don't like change. So, they "white knuckle" it and try to hold on to the "good old days" because they are afraid of new things on the horizon that will not be as good as the things in the past.

But here's what we know to be true—we have to move beyond just *white fists* and *black knuckles*. We can't afford to have the race conversation from just one perspective. We need open-handed conversations about race and opportunities to discuss relevant issues in the church from both a *black* and *white* perspective. Our call as Christians is to love all people, and we can't do that with closed fists. Racial diversity in the church is an opportunity to open our hands instead of an obstacle. We need to learn how to open our hands and surrender.

Consider

If you or any of your fellow group members do not know one another, take a few minutes to introduce yourselves. Then, to get things started, discuss one of the following questions:

- What opportunities have you had lately to talk about God and race?

— *or* —

- How has your church recently addressed conversations about race and faith?

Read

Invite someone to read aloud the following passage. Listen for new insights as you hear the verses being read, and then discuss the questions that follow.

Dear friends, let us love one another, for love comes from God. Everyone who loves has been born of God and knows God. Whoever does not love does not know God, because God is love. This is how God showed his love among us: He sent his one and only Son into the world that we might live through him. This is love: not that we loved God, but that he loved us and sent his Son as an atoning sacrifice for our sins. Dear friends, since God so loved us, we also ought to love one another. No one has ever seen God; but if we love one another, God lives in us and his love is made complete in us. . . .

God is love. Whoever lives in love lives in God, and God in them. This is how love is made complete among us so that we will have confidence on the day of judgment: In this world we are like Jesus. There is no fear in love. But perfect love drives out fear, because fear has to do with punishment. The one who fears is not made perfect in love.

We love because he first loved us. Whoever claims to love God yet hates a brother or sister is a liar. For whoever does not love their brother and sister, whom they have seen, cannot love God, whom they have not seen. And he has given us this command: Anyone who loves God must also love their brother and sister.

— 1 John 4:7–12, 16–21

What does this passage say about everyone who is in the family of God?

What does this passage have to do with how we approach the topic of racism?

Watch

Play the video segment for session one (see the streaming video access provided on the inside front cover). As you watch, use the following outline to record any thoughts or concepts that stand out to you.

God cares about *race*. We have different skin colors, speak different languages, enjoy different cultures, and yet the Bible says we are all human beings made in the image of God.

What is standing in our way of getting to where we need to go? *Clenched fists.* We hold onto the past, but we must be willing to receive with open hands.

The *black fist* is a symbol of standing up against the residue of segregation, slavery, and the systematic oppression that was (and still is) happening against black people in our country.

White knuckles is the other side of that equation. Many white Americans are still gripping to a long-standing paradigm of privilege that holds an advantage over people of color.

There are three big problems that result in us keeping our fists clenched:

  The pain problem: the pain of racism

The paralysis problem: the failure to stand up to racism by saying *that's enough!*

The perfection problem: perfection as a prerequisite for progress as it relates to racism

The Pharisees in Jesus' day were the original cancel culture. There is a story in John 8 where they catch a woman in adultery. They demanded perfection from her, but since she fell short, she sat paralyzed in fear in the temple courts—until Jesus entered the picture.

One day every tribe, tongue, and nation will be worshiping together. Until that day comes, our job is to work to make that a reality today. And we can't do that with closed fists.

Discuss

Take a few minutes with your group members to discuss what you just watched, and then explore these concepts in Scripture.

1. What stood out to you from listening to John and Wayne today? How can you identify with the stories they shared?

2. In what ways have problems caused by clenched fists—either *black fists* or *white knuckles*—shaped your own story? Which problem is most prevalent for you—the problem of pain, the problem of paralysis, or the problem of perfection?

3. The Bible gives us a beautiful picture of the beginning and end of the human story in Genesis 1:26–31 and Revelation 7:9–17. What stands out to you in these verses and gives you hope about the beginning and the end of our story?

4. Read Luke 10:25–37. There is a poignant reason that the story is called "The Good Samaritan" rather than "The Good Person." How is this story a challenge for us today? Can you think of a modern-day example?

5. Why do you think it is so hard for us to open our hands when it comes to the conversation on racism? What do we miss by keeping our fists clenched?

6. What will you do to stay engaged and open to challenges throughout this study? What specific commitment will you make to your group today?

Respond

Review the outline for the video teaching and any notes you took. In the space below, write down your most significant takeaway from this session.

Pray

One of the most important things you can do together in community is to pray for each other. This is not simply a closing prayer to end your group time but a portion of time to share prayer requests, review how God has answered past prayers, and actually pray for one another. As you close your time together this week, thank God for creating every tribe and nation in his image and for loving *all* of us as his children. Ask him to search your heart and give you that kind of love toward others, especially when they look different than you. And ask God to help you keep an open mind and open hands regarding this conversation on God and race over the next few sessions. Use the space below to record prayer requests and praises.

Name   Request/Praise

_____   _____

_____   _____

_____   _____

_____   _____

_____   _____

_____   _____

_____   _____

BETWEEN-SESSIONS PERSONAL STUDY

Reflect on the material you have covered during this week's group time by engaging in the following personal studies. Each day offers a short reading adapted from *God and Race*, along with a few reflection questions to take you deeper into the theme of this week's study. (You may also want to review chapters 1–3 in the book before you begin.) Be sure to read the reflection questions and make a few notes in your guide about the experience. At the start of your next group session, you will have a few minutes to share any insights that you learned.

Day One: The Pain of Racism

Read Genesis 32:22–32 and Matthew 11:25–30.

If you've ever experienced racism, you know how bad it hurts. When Wayne was just eight years old and living in the Bronx, he watched a white teenager call his mom the N-word and throw a rock that hit his mother in the back. He could tell it hurt her because she grimaced in pain when it happened. But she just looked over at Wayne and said in her deep, calm Jamaican voice, "Don't worry, jus' keep walkin,' babee." As an eight-year-old boy, Wayne was angry, confused, and sad all at once. The way his mother responded was one of the most important lessons of his life. She responded like a champion when she felt the pain of those rocks of racism—like a seasoned veteran taking the high road once again.

Unfortunately, Wayne's story has happened millions of times, in millions of different ways, to millions of different people. From microaggressions to blatant acts of racism, our nation has experienced deeply rooted racism since day one. Every time we turn on the news or open social media, it seems there is *another* story of blatant racism. Only now it's in plain view, caught on camera for everyone to see. And each incident hurts. It's no wonder open-handed conversations about race are so tricky when the pain of "racism rocks" is so real.

Persevering through the pain is not easy. Suffer enough pain, and you will eventually lose your willingness to engage. Experience enough hurt, and you will be tempted to stop showing up—or you will show up beaten down, with bruises and clenched fists. We have to keep walking and keep moving forward if we don't want to be paralyzed by our pain. We persevere through the pain of racism when we're willing to open our closed fists and be honest in conversation about our experience of *God and race.*

1. Have you ever had the "rocks" of racism hurled at you? Or have you ever watched someone throw rocks of racism at someone else? What happened?

2. Jacob walked around with a limp after a night of wrestling with God (see Genesis 32:22–32). He was no stranger to lifelong

pain, just like those of us who have experienced the lifelong pain of racism. How has the pain of racism affected you or the ones you love?

3. If you haven't experienced the pain of racism, do you understand why? How has the color of your skin or your life experience protected you from this pain?

4. What past experiences make you clench your fist and cause you to feel a sense of pain? How do the words of Jesus in Matthew 11:28 comfort you regarding this pain? How does the promise of Jesus allow you to keep moving forward despite the pain?

Talk to God about the pain of racism you've experienced in your life or the pain you've witnessed at the expense of others. Ask God to give you the courage to stay open-handed and willing to have hard conversations about the pain of racism with your community and church.

Day Two: The Problems of Racism

Read John 8:1–11 and Colossians 3:12–17.

White people are often nervous about whether it's better to say "black" or "African-American" because one wrong word could ruin you in the current age of cancel culture. But semantics are an obstacle to the crucial conversation we all need to be having. Saying the exact right thing is not as crucial as entering into a relationship and jumping into the conversation on God and race. As long as perfection with our words is a prerequisite for progress, we will stay paralyzed. Accountability is important, but open-handed conversations about race cannot happen where cancel culture abounds in both black and white communities.

Wayne, as a black pastor leading a racially diverse church, often faces this tension. If he doesn't address certain issues at just the right moment, the concern is that the black community will jump online and talk about how he's not *"woke"* enough. Or, if he doesn't phrase things just the right way, that the white community will Tweet about how he's part of the problem. Even worse, people from either side of the conversation on race will leave his church and make the desire for diversity even more difficult. But Wayne keeps moving forward in the conversation on God and race with an open hand because he wants an atmosphere conducive to healthy relationships and healthy conversations.

The pain of racism played out in either paralysis or perfection can make anyone want to throw in the towel and stop fighting for diversity. It's in those moments when we realize we've settled down with a group of people who look just like us and call it a day on the idea of diversity. But we must keep moving forward. We must look for similarities with those who are different from us, rather than get tripped up on semantics. We don't have time to let awkward, less-than-perfect interactions or past mistakes paralyze us if unity is the goal.

1. When you search your heart, what fears do you have about addressing this issue?

2. Have you canceled anybody recently, whether online or in person? If so, what was your motivation—panic, power, or something else?

3. Critiquing and canceling others is a convenient way for people to avoid their pain. But the beautiful and brilliant thing about Jesus is that he loves us too much to let us fall into that trap! Jesus may not have agreed with the Pharisees in the story told in John 8, but he never wrote them off. Rather, he engaged them in conversation. How does Jesus model this idea of dealing with people rather than dismissing them?

4. How can you do the same? How can you let the "peace of Christ rule in your hearts" (Colossians 3:15) by walking with someone or listening to them instead of canceling them when you disagree?

· Talk to God about the paralysis or the need for perfection you've experienced regarding conversations around racism. Ask God to give you the courage to keep engaging in conversation and keep working toward unity in diversity in your life and your church community.

Day Three: Keep on Walking

Read 2 Corinthians 12:1–10 and Hebrews 11:1–40.

If you're looking for a quick fix to your discomfort around the conversation on racism, you've come to the wrong place. This study isn't a quick fix. Rather, it's a *guide* that offers something better than fast solutions and quick fixes. It offers space to acknowledge your pain, paralysis, and imperfections, and *hope* for the future. It's meant to help you get back up and keep walking the walk and talking the talk even when it hurts—*especially when it hurts*.

Now, we are *not* suggesting you become walking target practice for those who commit racist acts of violence. But we *are* suggesting you keep moving forward with God in the midst of those acts, because God is your source of strength. Faith isn't weakness, and open-handed conversations about race are not for the faint of heart, so you'll need all the strength you can get. Walking with God will allow you to walk *through* the pain of systemic racism rather than running away from it and denying unhealthy reactions of perfection or paralysis.

We know that we have a lot of gumption to come along and tell everyone to just get along—to simply open their hearts and their hands regarding conversations on race. But we assure you, there are no easy ways for a bunch of imperfect people to fix centuries of pain and paralysis. Instead, this is an invitation to join the journey and keep walking. Just like Wayne's mother kept walking as those boys taunted her and threw a rock at her, we need to keep walking too. Walking paves the best path toward what we should be walking toward.

So, we are going to have to keep walking on the path toward conversations on *God and race* with open hands and open hearts if we want to know where we *should* be walking. When in doubt, keep on walking. And it's even better if we keep on walking together.

1. What makes it hard for you to keep walking on the journey of racial reconciliation? Where do you need a guide?

2. What invitations have you received from others and from God to keep walking this journey? How has God shown you his strength?

3. As you read Paul's words in 2 Corinthians 12:1–10, what reasons does he give for delighting in his weakness? Like Paul, how can you rely on God's grace and power in light of the reality of racism?

4. The author of Hebrews gives us a list of faith-filled people of God, all of whom had to keep walking when life got hard. Pick two or three people who stand out to you. In what ways was their weakness turned to strength?

Talk to God about what makes it so challenging for you to keep walking with open hands on the journey toward racial reconciliation and unity. Ask God for the strength you need—his strength—when you feel weak along the way.

Day Four: Standing Up Against Racism

Read Matthew 5:1–12 and Matthew 21:1–13.

We all know the feeling we get when our house isn't in order and someone comes over to visit. We are quick to speak up in those moments about our messy kids or busy schedule or lack of storage. We feel this way about our home because we take personal responsibility for our space. But are we willing to do the same when racism is the reason that things are out of order in our churches and in our communities?

Unfortunately, far too many Christians have remained silent about racism for far too long. So many of us are content to say *good enough* instead of *that's enough*. We feel like it's *good enough* we aren't racist or don't hang out with racist people—but *good enough* is not enough. We are God's plan for racial reconciliation as the church, yet we are hesitant to stand up and say something when others are treated like they don't matter. We're hesitant because we're afraid of what it will cost us. Perhaps this is because the moments when we stand up and say *that's enough* are expensive. History shows those moments can cost us our reputation, friendships, our job, even sometimes our lives. For Jesus, it cost him all of those things.

When Jesus rode into Jerusalem on Palm Sunday and found the court outside the temple filled with vendors and money changers, his response was costly. The temple was supposed to be a place of prayer for everyone. But the Jewish people of Jesus' day were intentionally blocking the Gentiles with vendors and money changing tables, making it nearly impossible for them to worship God. Blocking the outside court to prevent people from worshiping was not a spiritual issue—it was a racial issue.

When Jesus saw what was happening, he stood up to them and overturned their tables as if to say *that's enough*. Now it's time for us to do the same. When we are willing to stand up against racism in our homes, in our communities, and in our churches, there will be breaking points that bring about change.

1. What experiences do you have of you or people around you sticking up for someone else by saying "that's enough"? How did that courage impact the situation?

2. What experiences do you have when you or others didn't stand up for what was right? How did the lack of courage impact the situation? What do you wish had happened?

3. The story told in Matthew 21 relates how Jesus overturned the tables of the money changers and the benches of those selling doves outside the temple court. What else do you notice about the story? What spaces, activities, or ideas need to be "overturned" in your church community today so that all are welcome to worship Jesus?

4. According to Jesus' words in Matthew 5, who should we be standing up for in the world? How should this impact our response to racism?

Talk to God about what makes it costly or fearful for you to stand up against racism. Ask God to show you the small, simple, and tangible ways that you can start exercising those muscles right now so that you're ready to stand up against racism when the cost is high.

Day Five: Standing Up Together

Read John 15:9–17 and John 21:15–25.

Before we talk about all the ways we can change the world as a church or a community, we first need to look inwardly as individuals. The journey to open-handed conversations about God and race begins in our hearts. But we can't always do this journey on our own. Most times, we need the presence and the accountability of a friend—one who is willing to tell us when we have food stuck between our front teeth, literally and figuratively. We need friends who are willing to point out when we've excluded people who look different than us for more of the same—around our dinner tables, in our leadership circles, and in our board rooms.

Learning to not only stand up against racism but represent real unified diversity in our lives will be a process for many of us, but we can do it because of the people who have come before us to pave the way. And we can do it because of friends who are willing to walk with us along the way. Take Wayne and John for example. On the outside, it might look odd to see a black guy and a white guy partnering together to pastor a network church located in two different places—and they've received their fair share of challenges from concerned friends for doing so. But they are united in purpose to do something great, something God-ordained in a racially fragmented nation, *together*. This is called spiritual friendship.

When two friends intentionally choose to connect at the soul level like this, not only are they standing up against racism together, but they are also elevating the conversation about God and race in their respective church communities. The real power in the fight against racism comes when we open our hands together. It comes when, side-by-side, we unclench our black fists and white knuckles and have open-handed conversations without muting our diversity or compromising our integrity.

1. Who are the soul-level friends who choose to love you the way you are and yet challenge you to change?

2. How have you changed your point of view regarding race or faith as a result of a spiritual friendship?

3. In John 15, Jesus gives several reasons why he calls the disciples his friends. What are those reasons? What do they reveal about Jesus and his perspective on the disciples?

4. Jesus also illustrates how he views his disciples as friends by appearing to them three times after his death. On the third time, as recorded in John 21, we see and hear how deeply connected Jesus was to his disciples by the way he interacted with Peter and the way he talked about John. What are the signs of soul-level spiritual friendship displayed by Jesus in this

passage? What challenge does Jesus give Peter? How has that challenge changed the trajectory of the church as we know it today?

Talk to God about your current friendships as you embrace the conversation on racial reconciliation with open hands. Ask God to show you the friends who are willing to stand up with you in the fight against racism. Or, if needed, ask God to bring new soul-level friends into your life who will stand up to racism with you in this season.

For Next Week

Use the space below to write any insights or questions that you want to discuss at the next group meeting. Before your next session, read chapters 4–7 in *God and Race*.

START IN YOUR HEART

Search me, God, and know my heart.

PSALM 139:23

Welcome

If you've ever built anything, you know it is important to have a good foundation. When there is a crack in the base, it only takes a little pressure for the whole thing to implode. The same is true of our society. We've seen the impact of these "cracks in the foundation" throughout our history, from Red Summer to the Civil Rights Movement to the riots and protests of 2020.

There are several ways that people tend to react when these events occur. The white-knuckle approach is to get angry and ask, *Why can't they get over it already?* The black-fist approach is to retaliate and ask, *Do you now feel the pain you've made me feel?* But the open-handed approach we've been discussing is to empathize and ask, *What is broken in the system causing all this pain to spill over? How can we course correct?*

The journey toward open hands in racial healing requires an open *heart*. It's easy to sit in the grandstands and throw stones at others—public figures, politicians, police, even the pastors we see committing blatant acts of racism. We'd rather keep our distance and blame people for the injustice in the world than face our own anxious thoughts and offensive ways. Having heart-felt, open-handed conversations is a challenge—and to have those conversations, we have to do internal work to heal what we haven't been willing to confront in our lives.

If we want to engage in open-handed conversations about God and race, we have to address our own black fists and white knuckles. We have to acknowledge the profiling that happens and see the privilege some of us have over others. When we do this, our hearts open and all the walls we've constructed begin to fall. When that happens, we find forgiveness.

Letting God work to expose the things hidden in our hearts is not comfortable, and taking personal responsibility for being part of the solution rather than the problem is easier said than done. But the journey toward racial healing must begin in our hearts, so we have to push through the pain and discomfort of racism to find our way back to love and forgiveness. Heart work is *hard* work . . . but it's so worth it!

Consider

If you or any of your group members are just getting to know one another, take a few minutes to introduce yourselves and share any insights you have from last week's personal study. Then, to kick things off, discuss one of the following questions:

- What kind of soul searching have you done since last week?

  — *or* —

- If all of the emotional "storage rooms" of your heart were labeled with one descriptive word per compartment, what would those words be?

Read

Invite someone to read aloud the following passage from Psalm 139:1–17, 23–24. Listen for new insights as you hear the verses being read, and then discuss the questions that follow.

> You have searched me, Lord,
>> and you know me.
> You know when I sit and when I rise;
>> you perceive my thoughts from afar.
> You discern my going out and my lying down;
>> you are familiar with all my ways.
> Before a word is on my tongue
>> you, Lord, know it completely.
> You hem me in behind and before,
>> and you lay your hand upon me.
> Such knowledge is too wonderful for me,
>> too lofty for me to attain.
>
> Where can I go from your Spirit?
>> Where can I flee from your presence?
> If I go up to the heavens, you are there;

if I make my bed in the depths, you
are there.
If I rise on the wings of the dawn,
if I settle on the far side of the sea,
even there your hand will guide me,

your right hand will hold me fast.

If I say, "Surely the darkness will hide me
and the light become night around me,"
even the darkness will not be dark to you;
the night will shine like the day,
for darkness is as light to you.

For you created my inmost being;
you knit me together in my mother's womb.
I praise you because I am fearfully and
wonderfully made;
your works are wonderful,
I know that full well.
My frame was not hidden from you
when I was made in the secret place,
when I was woven together in the depths of
the earth.
Your eyes saw my unformed body;
all the days ordained for me were written
in your book
before one of them came to be. . . .

Search me, God, and know my heart;
test me and know my anxious thoughts.

See if there is any offensive way in me,
and lead me in the way everlasting.

What does the psalmist acknowledge about himself and about God?

What does it mean to ask God to "search" your heart? What would that involve?

Watch

Play the video segment for session two (see the streaming video access provided on the inside front cover). As you watch, use the following outline to record any thoughts or concepts that stand out to you.

This session is where the hard work begins because it is where the heart work begins.

The major issues surrounding race including profiling, privilege, and forgiveness:

Profiling is predicting someone's behavior based on a pre-conceived prejudice. It is making judgments about a certain person based on his or her skin color.

Privilege refers to inherent advantages possessed by white people on the basis of their race in a society characterized by racial inequality and injustice.

Forgiveness is what is required to move forward toward racial healing. We look to Jesus, who went to the cross for the very people who were putting nails through his hands.

There is no formula for forgiveness. You just keep forgiving and forgiving until you feel like you can't forgive anymore, and then you forgive again.

This idea causes Jesus' disciples to be overwhelmed and ask him to increase their faith. Jesus told them instead that they needed to start exercising the faith they already had.

Mulberry trees were known for having deep roots—removing them was incredibly challenging. Unforgiveness works the same way. The roots run deep and uprooting them is a process.

Discuss

Take a few minutes with your group members to discuss what you just watched, and then explore these concepts in Scripture.

1. What stood out to you from listening to John and Wayne today? How can you identify with the stories they shared?

2. Describe your reaction to the two exercises in this session. How many fingers did you have standing after the first exercise? How many after the second? What did you notice about yourself or the group after these exercises?

3. What's going on in your heart as you listen to this session? Are you angry, defensive, or, as the psalmist writes in Psalm 139:23–24, are there any offensive ways in you?

4. How have you contributed to or experienced the pain of pro-filing and privilege? What would it take for you to bear good fruit and forgive those who have hurt you—or forgive yourself for hurting others and release the guilt you feel?

5. **Read Luke 23:22–43.** How does Jesus model empathy on the cross toward those who hated him in the midst of excruciating pain? In what ways have you experienced or expressed radical forgiveness like this?

6. Jesus didn't run away from the pain; he ran through it. And Isaiah 53 reminds us that by his wounds, we are healed. How will you let forgiveness penetrate your pain? What step will you take this week to stay open-hearted in the wounded areas of your life?

Respond

Review the outline for the video teaching and any notes you took. In the space below, write down your most significant takeaway from this session.

Pray

Pray as a group before you close your time together. Thank God for the faith you've been given to take action in areas where you feel defensive and uncomfortable. Thank God for modeling ultimate forgiveness and empathy through the life and death of Jesus. Ask God to search your heart and see if there is any offensive way in you and reveal the places where you need to repent. And ask God to give you the strength to forgive others in light of the conversation on God and race. Use the space below to keep track of prayer requests and group updates.

Name   Request/Praise

_____   _____

_____   _____

_____   _____

_____   _____

_____   _____

_____   _____

_____   _____

BETWEEN-SESSIONS PERSONAL STUDY

Reflect on the material you covered during this week's group time by engaging in the following personal studies. Each day offers a short reading adapted from *God and Race*, along with a few reflection questions to take you deeper into the theme of this week's study. Be sure to read the reflection questions and make a few notes in your guide about the experience. At the start of your next session, you will have a few minutes to share any insights that you learned.

Day One: Understanding Profiling

Read Psalm 30:1–12; Lamentations 3:17–33; and Matthew 5:43–48.

You've probably heard stories of profiling similar to the one Wayne shared. As uncomfortable as these stories are, we must not only talk about them but also allow ourselves to *feel* the sadness, confusion, and pain these injustices cause. Grievously, many black people experience profiling on a regular basis. Every movement matters, and every response has to be methodical.

An important step in the process is *believing* the stories of profiling. Profiling is suffocating, stifling, and feels like a proverbial knee holding a person down. If we keep glossing over the tragedies that happen as a result of profiling, we'll keep repeating them. So, whether you're hearing stories for the first time or the hundredth time, take a few moments to believe them and feel the weight of them. Racism is real and profiling is a problem because it reduces humans to stereotypes. This doesn't mean crimes should go unpunished, but it does mean that everyone who commits a crime deserves the right to go to jail, stand trial, and be treated like a human being rather than lose his or her life at the point of a shotgun or under someone's knee.

It's also important to understand the *pain* of profiling. If you've been surrounded by or have been the victim of racism for years, there's a good chance you've gone numb to it. This is called *apathy*, and it's one of the protective ways our body copes with pain. When the pain gets too bad, it shuts off all feelings and we go numb. But the heart check is to make sure we haven't gone numb to experiencing, watching, or contributing to this kind of pain. As much as it hurts, feeling the pain of profiling is a gift because it means we're awake to what's going on around us. It means we *feel the burn* of what profiling does to us as humans and as a society. And when we're awake to it, we are more prone to take action.

But action isn't everything. We must also *lament* and mourn our experiences together. Scripture reminds us we are in good company when doing so. Throughout the stories of the Bible, God invites us to process injustice and pain, and even get angry with him, by *lamenting*. When we learn to lament, then we can change. Heart change happens when we trust each other and God enough to process injustice and pain together. That's the power of feeling the burn of racism together.

1. What is going on in your heart when you think about stories of profiling? What emotions do you feel similar to King David in

Psalm 30—apathy, anger, hopelessness, sadness? How can you express your emotions in a healthy way with trusted people?

2. Lamenting is a way of mourning and processing the pain of racial injustice. What do you see in Lamentations 3:17–33 as you read about Israel's lamenting and God's presence with them? What does it look like for you to mourn the reality of injustice today?

3. What are you doing to stay awake to the reality of profiling? How do you make a point to listen to the stories of people who have experienced it on a real and consistent basis?

4. How will you be a part of the solution when it comes to profiling? In what ways can you commit to standing up for your brothers and sisters who experience profiling on a real and consistent basis? How will you pray for those who contribute to the pain of persecution (see Matthew 5:43–48)?

Talk to God about the pain of profiling. If you've gone numb, ask God to help you feel again. If you've never experienced it, ask God to give you eyes to see and ears to listen. Pray that the Lord will break your heart for what breaks his heart.

Day Two: Acknowledging Privilege

Read Isaiah 58:1–12; Matthew 22:1–10; and Matthew 22:34–40.

Privilege may be an uncomfortable topic to talk about, but it's foundational for learning how to have conversations about race. If you're white and live in America, the reality is that there are certain advantages you've enjoyed throughout your life that you didn't have to earn. This is called *white privilege*, and it means "inherent advantages possessed by a white person on the basis of their race in a society characterized by racial inequality and injustice."

As mentioned in this session, this doesn't mean that your life has been easy. It doesn't mean you haven't worked hard for the things you have. And it doesn't mean you haven't had your own experiences of poverty, persecution, and problems. It just means your skin color hasn't been one of those problems. You haven't had to consider how your skin color impacts your life on a day-to-day or minute-by-minute basis the way a person of color has had to do.

Talking about white privilege isn't meant to shame you for being white, or invalidate your life experiences, or devalue your accomplishments. It's meant to stir up awareness of the stark contrast of privilege available to you simply because of the color of your skin, and it's meant to promote empathy in conversations with people of color in your community. Being white is not your fault, but it does give you an advantage. That's why it's crucial to lower your defenses if you're white and learn to keep a soft heart while talking about privilege.

A great place to start in acknowledging white privilege is to actually notice the privileges you've been given over others of color. With your privilege, you can then start to give others privilege: a seat at the table, a voice in the room, a spot on the team, a place in the pulpit. Also, it's important to acknowledge that you were likely taught a version of history that doesn't represent the total picture. Our history books, our classrooms, and our educational institutions tend to be based on a white perspective. And if the only history we learn is limited in scope, lacking subject matter on the topic of slavery and glossing over the impact of the Jim Crow era, how can we accurately learn to empathize with the pain of an entire group of people?

Feeling bad about your skin color isn't the point. Shame is not helpful. Action is. Acknowledging your privilege means you get to do something productive with what you have.

1. What does *privilege* mean to you? Why is it important to acknowledge that privilege exists in our country today?

2. In Isaiah 58, the prophet called out the privilege of the Israelites in the context of a story on fasting. How does he encourage the Israelites to use their privilege (see verses 6–10)? How can you start stewarding your privilege, no matter the color of your skin?

3. What does the parable of the wedding banquet in Matthew 22:1–10 reveal about Jesus' thoughts on privilege? What new insight do you notice about this passage when you read it in light of privilege and the conversation on God and race?

4. How does the Great Commandment that Jesus issues in Matthew 22:34–40 shape your response to privilege? What responsibilities can you step into publicly and privately to make sure everyone around you has access to the same privileges as you do?

Talk to God about the discomfort of acknowledging your privilege or the anger at your lack of privilege. Ask God for a soft and surrendered heart as you steward the responsibility you have to use your privilege for the good of others or the responsibility you have to lovingly remind your friends of the privilege they carry in the world.

Day Three: Embracing the Pain

Read Acts 7:51–60; Acts 9:1–31; and Philippians 3:13–14.

If there is one thing that's clear as we listen to the hymns of our African-American ancestors like "Hold On" and "Swing Low Sweet Chariot," it's this: *they had a resilient spirit.* Their strength didn't come from running away from their pain. It came from running *through* it. They embraced their pain as they sang about it and kept moving forward with their eyes set on the promised land of freedom. We must *continue* learning from the past and keep telling our painful stories if we're ever going to find healing on the journey of racial reconciliation. And we can do so while simultaneously lamenting, feeling the pain, and letting go of the bitterness in our hearts.

But this is the hard part: instead of pretending to forget the pain, we need to face it and find forgiveness for those who caused it. It's not about getting amnesia about the past. It's about acknowledging the pain and running straight into it so we can truly learn to love our enemies. Pain doesn't always mean physical pain like Wayne's story of the rocks thrown at his mother. It can pile up in the form of well-meaning (yet hurtful) comments, a cold shoulder, an off-color joke. Pain is real. But we can respond to our pain by taking a lesson from the story of Stephen, who gazed upward toward heaven in the midst of his pain. When we learn to look to Jesus in our pain, then we begin to act more like Jesus to the world, too. When you and I are most rejected and burnt by racism, Jesus makes it clear that we are most received in heaven. Like Stephen, we can learn to glance at our pain, while at the same time, gazing at heaven.

If you grew up in the church, you know how much Christians love to celebrate Paul's conversion story in Acts 9. But think about the baggage he had to work through afterward and all the shame and guilt of the pain he caused by persecuting other people. Truth is, we all have pain in our past. We may not have been killing people like Paul did and throwing them in prison for thinking differently than us, but we've all said and done some things we wish we could take back. Just like Paul, we may be experiencing the pain of regret for our past. But there is promise in our future. And we take hold of that promise when we're willing to forgive others and ourselves. As we've said before, our pain is a gift when we can see how it shapes the way we show up in the present and how it inspires us to keep moving forward toward racial healing.

1. What kind of pain has racism caused in your life? Were you the giver of that pain or the receiver of that pain? What other emotions surface alongside your pain?

2. Up until now, what have you done with that pain? Have you stuffed it, expressed it in outrage or anger, ignored it, felt weighed down by the guilt and shame of it? How do the stories of Stephen and Paul inspire you to release that pain and give it to God?

3. Paul wrote that he was "forgetting what is behind" and pressing on "toward the goal" (Philippians 3:13–14). Why is it important to move beyond the shame of the past?

4. Is there someone in your life with whom you can share your pain—a trusted friend or someone who comes from a different background and perspective? How will you make it a priority to share your pain with them this week?

Talk to God about the pain you've given or experienced as a result of racism. Ask God for the courage to walk straight into your pain, knowing that he will be with you. Thank God for the healing that comes when you acknowledge your pain and for the tender scar that reminds you of how far you've come on the journey.

Day Four: The Art of Forgiveness

Read Isaiah 43:14–21; Matthew 18:21–35; and Ephesians 4:32.

The old adage *forgive and forget* sounds great, but is it really the best strategy? Do we ever really forget the pain we've experienced, especially when it comes in the form of systemic racism? You can't heal from centuries of pain by pretending it never happened. If you want to heal *for real*, you have to learn the art of forgiveness—which is way harder than it sounds, especially in a culture that expends so much energy running away from forgiveness.

Those who forget the past are bound to repeat it. For black people, that means we have to forgive white people of previous and present injustices. And we have to do it while not harboring hatred and racism toward them. Those words might be a little unsettling to you. But that's the point. If you want to be a voice that fights for racial healing, you have to learn and practice the art of forgiveness. Nothing echoes louder throughout the hallways of history than unforgiveness. When we refuse to forgive, we just continue to repeat our pain.

Forgiving doesn't mean that you forget. It means you choose to let go of the anger, ill intent, or resentment you feel toward the person or thing that caused you pain. When you're ready to release those feelings, God is prepared to step into your heart where you've been storing your bitterness and fill it with forgiveness and his presence.

Forgiveness will not always make sense. Just look at the forgiveness extended by Jesus while he was hanging on the cross. He forgave those who wrongly accused him, tortured him, and were in the process of killing him. This means we can forgive the very people and systems contributing to the disparities we see in the landscape of racial justice. Forgiveness may not have a formula, but it will always set you free. And we learn the art of forgiveness by practicing forgiveness day by day, one act at a time.

1. Have you ever had to forgive the same person or system "seventy times seven" (see Matthew 18:22), meaning, "again and again," for the same offense? What else makes forgiveness especially hard for you?

2. Do you have anyone in your life who sounds like a broken record of bitterness? Who are the people in your life who regularly practice forgiveness and live like the picture you see in Isaiah 43:21—like God is always up to something new?

3. Jesus exhaled powerful words of forgiveness from the cross. How has someone else's forgiveness shaped your life for the better? What does it feel like to be forgiven for a wrong you committed— whether that wrong was intentional or unintentional?

4. What kind of forgiveness do you need to practice today as you choose to be kind? Do you need to forgive a person who has inflicted pain on you? Do you need to forgive yourself (or even forgive God) for the ways you feel like you have been let down?

Talk to God about what it takes to let go of the bitterness you've been harboring and to forgive just as God forgave you. Ask Jesus to increase your faith as you practice the art of forgiveness so you can see the new work God is doing in you and around you.

Day Five: Practicing Humility and Hope

Read Matthew 6:5–15; Luke 18:9–14; and Acts 13:38–52.

Hopefully, by now we all want to become the type of people who fight for racial justice for the right reasons—not just when we're trying to avoid criticism or react to a crisis. While there is a time and place for those short-term responses, the ultimate goal is to respond with a healthy heart out of a deep conviction that *racism is wrong.* And if we want a healthy heart toward one another in our response to racial justice, we have to start practicing healthy habits.

The first requirement for practicing healthy habits is *humility.* We start with humility because it's fertile ground for reconciliation. Take Paul, for example. No matter how high he rose in the early church, he never forgot how low he began. Paul hated people who didn't think the same way as him when he was Saul, the Jewish Pharisee. But Paul's humility in being quick to admit that he was wrong allowed him to make such a drastic change after his conversion. Eventually, Paul's humility is what paved the way for the gospel to spread beyond the Jews to the Gentile world. He is one of the primary reasons the good news of Jesus spread to the ends of the earth. Paul wasn't just humble—he was *hopeful* as well.

Humility leads us to have open hands, open minds, and open hearts on the journey toward racial justice. Humility is the reason we can have honest conversations about privilege, profiling, and forgiveness. Humble hearts trade in black fists and white knuckles for flags of surrender. And humble hearts remain hopeful of the new work God is going to do. Humility and hope are ultimately the reasons we can be agents of reconciliation, just like Jesus and just like Paul. So keep praying, keep reaching out, and keep hoping. No one is too far gone for God.

1. Can you name some examples of how a lack of humility has derailed efforts on the journey toward racial justice? Just like the story of the Pharisee and the tax collector in Luke 18:9–14, what makes humility a struggle for you at times?

2. How will you follow the example Jesus gave in Matthew 6:5–15—practicing humility on a regular basis? What other healthy habits require practice in your life?

3. What signs do we see in Acts 13:38–52 that Paul and Barnabas remained humble and hopeful as they preached the gospel and were challenged by the Jewish leaders of the day? How

does this story motivate you toward humility and hope in your situation?

4. How will you practice humility and hope as means to a healthy heart in the conversation about God and race? In what ways can these habits help you to "guard your heart above all else" (Proverbs 4:23)?

Talk to God about your desire to practice humility and hope as healthy heart habits. Ask God to give you the discipline required to make these habits a consistent practice in your life. Close out your time with God by praying the Lord's Prayer from Matthew 6:9–13.

For Next Week

Use the space below to write any insights or questions that you want to discuss at the next group meeting. Before your next session, read chapters 8–9 in *God and Race*.

WHAT ABOUT YOUR HOME?

God does not show favoritism but
accepts from every nation the one who
fears him and does what is right.

ACTS 10:34–35

Welcome

Does everyone in your social circle look like you? If so, it's
time to make new friends and expand your circle of diver-
sity. Here's why: *It's no accident you live in this place and time.* From the
beginning, God had a plan for your life.

We all grew up in different households, and the home we
grew up in shaped our lives—for better or worse—and now
we have homes and households to shape. We are building the

households that future generations will grow up in and learn from, and that makes us history-makers. We get to establish the kind of households where unity is the rule and racism is rare . . . where racial healing is the reality instead of a far-off dream. But we have to take responsibility for building these kinds of households and communities.

History is calling us forward to play our part in having open-handed conversations about race *in our homes*, not just in our churches, corporations, or places where we go to learn. If we want to create churches that look like heaven, we must take an honest look at the way we create space for diversity in our homes. Often, we refuse to do so and throw stones at our churches instead. We'd rather look at the faults of racism and division anywhere else than in the place we reside. So, it's crucial to ask ourselves, *what type of home do we want our children and their children to inherit?* The homes we build, the social circles we swim in, and the things we post online as a result of those social connections matter.

In this session, we will begin to focus outward and talk about our households. As we do, we have to remember that fighting for diversity is a process—a process where we strive for progress, not perfection. Moving beyond black fists and white knuckles takes *time*, and consistency in those conversations is key. The best way to break down walls is to invite people to walk through the door and build a household that looks like heaven.

Consider

Begin your group time by inviting those in the group to share their insights from last week's personal study. Then, to kick things off, discuss one of the following questions:

- What are a few ways you engage with people who come from a different culture than you do?

— *or* —

- How do you invite diversity into your home?

Read

Invite someone to read aloud the following passage: Acts 10:9–28. Listen for new insights as you hear the verses being read, and then discuss the questions that follow.

About noon the following day as they [Cornelius, the centurion, along with two servants and a soldier] were on their journey [to find Peter] and approaching the city, Peter went up on the roof to pray. He became hungry and wanted something to eat, and while the meal was being prepared, he fell into a trance. He saw heaven opened and something like a large sheet being let down to earth by its four corners. It contained all kinds of four-footed animals, as well as reptiles and birds. Then a voice told him, "Get up, Peter. Kill and eat."

"Surely not, Lord!" Peter replied. "I have never eaten anything impure or unclean."

The voice spoke to him a second time, "Do not call anything impure that God has made clean."

This happened three times, and immediately the sheet was taken back to heaven.

While Peter was wondering about the meaning of the vision, the men sent by Cornelius found out where Simon's house was and stopped at the gate. They called out, asking if Simon who was known as Peter was staying there.

While Peter was still thinking about the vision, the Spirit said to him, "Simon, three men are looking for you. So get up and go downstairs. Do not hesitate to go with them, for I have sent them."

Peter went down and said to the men, "I'm the one you're looking for. Why have you come?"

The men replied, "We have come from Cornelius the centurion. He is a righteous and God-fearing man, who is respected by all the Jewish people. A holy angel told him to ask you to come to his house so that he could hear what you have to say." Then Peter invited the men into the house to be his guests.

The next day Peter started out with them, and some of the believers from Joppa went along. The following day he arrived in Caesarea. Cornelius was expecting them and had called together his relatives and close friends. As Peter entered the house, Cornelius met him and fell at his feet in reverence. But Peter made him get up. "Stand up," he said, "I am only a man myself."

While talking with him, Peter went inside and found a large gathering of people. He said to them: "You are well aware that it is against our law for a Jew to associate with or visit a Gentile. But God has shown me that I should not call anyone impure or unclean."

What was God revealing to Peter through the vision he experienced?

What conclusions did Peter reach about the way he had been treating Gentiles?

Watch

Play the video segment for session three (see the streaming video access provided on the inside front cover). As you watch, use the following outline to record any thoughts or concepts that stand out to you.

Before we talk about the church, we have to talk about inviting diversity into our own homes. What type of home will our children and their children inherit?

Sometimes the best way to break down walls is to invite people to walk through the door.

A diverse group of people + a welcoming environment that empha- sizes working together + a common goal or mission = success

Five **STEPS** to help you build diversity into our communities:

Speak up

Take personal responsibility

Educate yourself

Pray

Start building diversity in your relationships

Food is one of the best ways to invite diversity into your home. Jesus knew this and constantly used this strategy. Reach out to friends and neighbors and invite them over for a meal.

Fighting for diversity is a process. Strive for progress . . . not perfection.

Discuss

Take a few minutes with your group members to discuss what you just watched, and then explore these concepts in Scripture.

1. What stood out to you from listening to John and Wayne today? How can you identify with the stories they shared?

2. When was the last time you invited a diverse group of people into your home? How was that time different from when you have your regular social circle over?

3. **Read Mark 14:1–26.** Have you ever noticed how many stories of Jesus happen around a table with a diverse group of people? What do you notice about the table stories found in this passage? How was Jesus' heart for diversity reflected here?

4. In Luke 10:38–42, we read about Mary and Martha and a moment with Jesus in their home. Why were Mary's actions so important to Jesus? How is this story a lesson for inviting people into our homes?

5. The story of Jesus inviting himself to the home of Zacchaeus (told in Luke 19:1–10) is more about Jesus' heart for diversity and less about looking for a good meal. Why was this a controversial move by Jesus? What did Zacchaeus represent to the Jews?

6. Which **STEPS** toward racial diversity have you been practicing in your own home? Which ones could use a little more work?

Respond

Review the outline for the video teaching and any notes you took. In the space below, write down your most significant takeaway from this session.

Pray

Pray as a group before you close your time together. Thank God for creating such diverse communities of people and for giving us peace in our hearts as we reach across racial lines for unity. Ask God to show you how your misconceptions of other people have kept you from entering into certain homes or opening your door to more people. And ask God to give you a spirit of confidence, calmness, collaboration, and consistency as you fight for diversity in your home. Use the space below to keep track of prayer requests and group updates.

Name   Request/Praise

_____   _____

_____   _____

_____   _____

_____   _____

_____   _____

_____   _____

BETWEEN-SESSIONS PERSONAL STUDY

Reflect on the material you covered during this week's group time by engaging in the following personal studies. Each day offers a short reading adapted from *God and Race*, along with a few reflection questions to take you deeper into the theme of this week's study. Be sure to read the reflection questions and make a few notes in your guide about the experience. At the start of your next session, you will have a few minutes to share any insights that you learned.

Day One: Speak Up

Read Joshua 2:1–16; Joshua 6:22–23; and Mark 10:46–52.

If you've ever felt unqualified to reach out to a hurting friend of another race, remember that *empathy is more important than eloquence.* You aren't going to get it perfect, but don't let the fear of saying the wrong thing hinder you from saying anything at all. You don't have to say anything tweetable or overtly poignant. When someone is hurting, they just need you to empathize. So don't feel that you have to be an expert scholar on all the racial problems before you jump in and have conversations. People need your questions more than your answers. Your presence in people's lives is more important than your solutions. Scary as it may sound, we promote what we stay silent about, so we have a responsibility to speak up!

The first key to building diversity in your home is confidence. Many people feel the pressure to code-switch—to change their behavior based on their surroundings. There is a pressure to just fit in and play the part. It's human nature. At times it feels so much simpler to be like everyone else. But it's not your job to fit into a certain mold—the mold, it seems, that the world is telling you to squeeze into. It's your job to have the confidence to be the person God created you to be. It's your job to speak up with confidence in the way God uniquely wired you.

The truth is that we are *all* children of the King, coheirs with Christ, created in the image of God. Remembering who we are gives us the confidence to speak up. If we're going to bring diversity into our homes in the way that God would desire, then we need to be the full expression of image-bearers of God. But we must be mindful of how we use our words. Left unchecked and combined with unhealthy emotions, our words can be dangerous to others. However, our words can also be incredibly healing and life-giving.

So, check yourself, and then have the confidence to use your words and speak up for what you believe God is telling you to be true regarding the role of diversity in your home.

1. How does Rahab's confidence to speak up to strangers who were different from her save her and her family? When have you had the confidence to speak up during a difficult or dangerous situation? What was the outcome?

2. How does Jesus respond when Bartimaeus speaks to him and his disciples with courage and confidence? In what ways might this situation have encouraged onlookers too?

3. What are some of the risks you have taken to speak up for others? What were some of the benefits and rewards you experienced for doing so?

4. How is God calling you to speak up and work toward diversity in your home?

Close out your time today by talking with God as you consider ways to contribute to a significant change in racial diversity by using your voice. Ask God to give you his peace and the confidence to speak up and be heard for the sake of others.

Day Two: Take Personal Responsibility

Read Luke 2:1–12; Matthew 2:1–12; and 2 Corinthians 5:17–21.

In this process of navigating open-handed conversations about race, we may not always get it right. When we miss it, it will be tempting for us to pass the buck. But we need to own our mistakes and commit to doing better next time. Blame is one of the great enemies of unity, for as long as we all refuse to take personal responsibility, we won't make any progress.

When we read the Gospels, it's clear that Jesus was a step ahead of everyone. He took responsibility for his own actions—as well as the actions of others when they were unwilling or unable to do so for themselves. When they persecuted him, he kept the peace. When Pilate questioned him, he remained calm. When he was being publicly crucified, he prayed for those who were punishing him. Jesus mastered this art and drew a diverse crowd around him. And that diverse crowd is what eventually became the start of the church.

Taking responsibility for racial reconciliation is one of the most important and liberating things that we can do. However, make no mistake, people will try to distort what we've said or disagree with our position on racial unity. But it's not our job to win popularity polls. It's our job to take personal responsibility for the racial injustices we see. It's not our job to make people happy. It's our job to keep this open-handed conversation moving forward. We are responsible for ourselves and what our social circle looks like. It's our job to invite diversity into our homes.

So let's not blame, pass the buck, or retreat when we don't get it right. Instead, let's commit to doing it better next time. The temptation to retreat into our homes as if they were our castles is real. We retreat, dig a moat, and pull up the drawbridge so that we can be the king and queen of our space. But God created us to be in community, and that includes taking responsibility for our actions and for inviting a diverse group of people into our space.

1. Have you ever considered how the context of the birth of Jesus, including the visitors he received at the moment and

afterward, shows us the significance of the diverse community he welcomed around him? What does this insight mean to you?

2. What are some ways you have seen people blame others for our current racial struggles? How might things be different if people took more personal responsibility?

3. What can you do to take personal responsibility on the journey toward more open-handed conversations regarding racial unity?

4. The Bible uses the term *reconciliation* to describe the type of unity that God wants us to have in the church. How did Jesus reconcile our relationship with God (see 2 Corinthians 5:17–21)? And how does he invite us to do the same?

Close out your time today by asking God to help you to consider the ways you can take responsibility for biblical reconciliation by inviting diversity into your home. May this be one of the most important and liberating things you do for the kingdom of God!

Day Three: Educate Yourself

Read Luke 2:41–52 and Matthew 23:1–12.

Let's get straight to the point today: *the quickest way to dishonor our commitment to advancing racial equity is to stop learning.* These days, we don't have any excuse to be uneducated about race. Yes, it's easy to criticize previous generations for how they handled race relations, and rightly so. But let's also remember that they didn't have as many resources (or social media) readily available to them as we do today. We live in a day and age where there is so much material on any given topic. However, too often, instead of opening a book, we let the talking heads from our favorite news media outlets tell us what we want to hear.

The only way to excel in education is to continue diving into books, podcasts, and videos, and listening to and learning from the experiences of others. And please, whatever you do to learn, don't just read people who confirm your beliefs but think critically and interact with the thoughts and opinions of others who are different from you. Remember, *some of the most spiritual people in the world might disagree with you.* When someone recommends a book to you, especially if they're of a different race, you have a massive opportunity to have an open-handed conversation regarding the perspectives that person is sharing with you.

When everyone in the room looks, thinks, and acts the same, it becomes way too easy for the "enlightened few" to create all the narratives. This is called *groupthink*, a phenomenon coined by psychologists, in which the elite few make decisions while discouraging creativity and critical thinking from the rest of the group. Collaboration is condemned in this kind of setting. But, as Maya Angelou once said, *when we know better, we do better.* This is why educating ourselves and learning from a diverse group of voices is of utmost importance.

1. How did Jesus model the importance of listening and learning at an early age (see Luke 2:41–52)? Notice the key phrase in verse 46—Jesus was "asking them questions." How does this passage inspire you to educate yourself and ask questions?

2. What questions have you asked lately to learn more about someone who has a different perspective than you do? If you haven't done so lately, who will you seek to listen and learn from— someone who is also a safe place to process your questions?

3. *Information informs and action transforms.* We must take action on what we discover when we educate ourselves. According to Jesus, where was the disconnect for the Pharisees (see Matthew 23:1–12)? How was their information informing their actions?

4. Why is it so important to think critically about a topic and interact with thoughts and opinions different from yours? How are you doing this on a consistent basis?

Close out your time today by asking God about the motives of your heart when it comes to educating yourself on racial equality, especially from voices who think differently than you do. Ask God to help you think more critically and to ask thoughtful questions on this journey.

Day Four: Pray

Read John 17:20–26; Acts 10:9–48; and Joshua 3:1–11.

The longer we are on the journey toward racial reconciliation, the more we realize that prayer has to be our starting point. Prayer is essential in bringing about unity, and unity is the secret to ending racism. So, we need to get back to prayer if we're ever going to move forward. Prayer is what allows us to be consistent in the journey toward racial diversity in our homes.

Racism, prejudice, bigotry, and oppression are all forms of sin. These are spiritual problems that require spiritual solutions. Long-held biases may not change overnight. Racist roots run deep and finding freedom is a process; it's a process of prayer that requires our consistent attention regularly. And we have a constant invitation to pray and see the world the way God designed it. Just as God laid a sheet in front of Peter in Acts 10, God is constantly inviting us to rise, pray, and see the world the way God designed it. Every day is a new opportunity to humble ourselves and pray, then get up and kill the prejudices that keep us from loving everyone, making disciples of all nations, and bringing diversity into our homes.

Life post-Covid seems a bit uncertain at times, especially when racial prejudice continues to be an ongoing pandemic. But we aren't the only ones to live and lead in a crazy season. The book of Joshua highlights the story of the wandering Israelites on their search for the Promised Land. After forty years, they were finally about to enter the land. But they were hesitant and nervous because there were a lot of unknowns. *Sound familiar?* The Israelites didn't have a roadmap, but they trusted Joshua's vision and his prayer life with God. Just as it did for Joshua, prayer reminds us to let God go first in our lives, and it empowers us to follow God's leading.

What if we developed the habit of stopping for five minutes every once in a while to ask God to continue leading us in the racial healing and restoration we so desperately need in the world? And what if we prayed that God would start with us and our homes? As you take time to pause and pray today, ask God to bring one diverse friendship into your life and give you the boldness to pursue and cultivate that friendship.

1. Jesus understood the power of prayer for himself and others even in his final moments leading up to the cross. What was his prayer for all believers as it relates to unity?

2. Just as God laid a sheet in front of Peter (see Acts 10:11), so God lays prayerful dreams and visions on our hearts and minds. What kind of specific vision or dream are you praying about as you bring more diversity into your home?

3. On the eve of entering the Promised Land, Joshua told the people to "consecrate" themselves because God was about to do amazing things among them. He basically asked them to prayerfully dedicate themselves to God. How are you likewise dedicating your heart and your home to God?

4. In what ways does your dedication to God motivate and challenge you to be a part of bringing spiritual solutions to the spiritual problems of racism? How will you work with others in your community to take crucial steps consistently toward racial equality?

Close out your time by asking God to lead you on this journey toward racial equity, beginning in your heart and in your home. Ask him to bring at least one diverse friendship into your life.

Day Five: Start Building Diversity in Your Relationships

Read Matthew 4:18–25; Matthew 9:9–13; Mark 3:16–19; and Acts 1:1–10.

It's important to be intentional about building diversity into your relationships—to reach out to people who are different from you, open up conversations on race, and listen and learn from them. But here's the key. The goal is not just to seek these connections so you can gain knowledge and learn from others. The goal is to build *friendships*. The people you invite into your lives are the means to an end. The friendship *is the end* in and of itself.

Food is one of the best ways to invite diversity into your home. It doesn't matter who you are or where you come from—we all need to eat. Food brings everyone together. Jesus knew this strategy well and constantly employed it to bring people together. You'll be amazed at how quickly and easily conversation about diverse experiences in life happens over delicious food on the table. But don't put pressure on this—the win with inviting people into your home and around your table is simply extending the invitation and enjoying the evening. You can even ask others to bring the food! If it goes well, then you can consider making it a monthly thing. You never know when a simple meal is going to turn into a lifelong friendship or when a simple act of kindness is going to have a ripple effect that outlasts your lifetime.

Always remember that *your actions matter*. They send out ripple effects into the world. You have no idea how far little acts of friendship will go, even when they don't seem like a big deal to you. Your home matters, you have influence in your social circle, and people will notice how you use your influence and your home. So, get up, get in the game, and use your voice for good. And don't just do this once. When you get through all five **STEPS**, repeat the process. It may sound like a lot of work, but before long, you will see your social circle start to change!

1. The disciples whom Jesus called to follow him came from a variety of diverse backgrounds. What does Matthew 4:18–25 reveal about the first group? What do you imagine would have been their standing in society?

2. What do you learn about the background of Matthew in Matthew 9:9–13? What did Jesus do in his friendship with him that drew the scorn of the Pharisees?

3. One of the disciples listed in Mark 3:16–19 is Simon the Zealot. The Zealots were a political party who sought to overthrow the occupying Roman government. (Remember that Matthew, as a tax collector, would have worked for the Romans.) What does this reveal about the type of people whom Jesus chose to be his friends?

4. How do the final words that Jesus spoke to his followers in Acts 1:1–10 reveal his heart for racial unity? What do you understand about the relationship between the places Jesus mentions—Jerusalem, Judea, Samaria, "and the ends of the earth"—and why was it important for the disciples to take the gospel to those places?

Close out your time by asking God about the motives of your heart as you build new friendships and bring people into your home. Pray that he will give you the courage to gather a diverse group of people together over good conversation and food.

For Next Week

Use the space below to write any insights or questions that you want to discuss at the next group meeting. Before your next session, read chapters 10–11 in *God and Race*.

USE YOUR INFLUENCE

Let everything you say be good and
helpful, so that your words will be an
encouragement to those who hear them.
EPHESIANS 4:29 NLT

Welcome

We all have influence on others at some level. If you are a parent, you have influence over your children. If you are a manager, you have influence over the people who report to you. If you are a close friend to another person, you have influence over that individual's life. The crucial question to consider when it comes to the topic of racial healing is whether we are using the influence we possess to be a part of the *solution* or a part of the problem.

We amp up opportunities to use our influence when we're willing to stay calm and be confident. Truth be told, when we lack confidence, people will have a hard time hearing us. We want to be pillars of truth and justice, but we have to have a firm and confident foundation to do so. This is why it's important for us to take cues from Jesus on this journey. Jesus was a pillar and foundation for the entire gospel. He set the example of what it means for us to be a part of the solution instead of the problem by showing up confidently and calmly on a consistent basis.

But Jesus also did this with *love*. We live in a day and age where our words have the power to influence others not just in person but online. This can be dangerous when we exchange pleasantries in person but then throw daggers at the individual when we're posting. We have to remember that people are always watching and that our platforms are a gift. With great power to listen and respond—both online and in person—comes great responsibility. And our great responsibility lies in the Greatest Commandment: *to love God and love others*.

As we will discuss in this session, wielding our influence isn't just about *what* we say but also about *how* we say it. We might be right about something, but if we don't say it in love . . . then we're in the wrong. As Paul put it, "If I speak in the tongues of men or of angels, but do not have love, I am only a resounding gong" (1 Corinthians 13:1). Without love, our words and posts are just white noise. This is how we move forward in the journey toward racial healing—*with open hearts, open hands, and words of influence and love*.

Consider

Begin your group time by inviting those in the group to share their insights from last week's personal study. Then, to kick things off, discuss one of the following questions:

- What three words would you use to describe the influence you have in your community or circle of friends?

— *or* —

- Think of someone who has influenced your life. How and why did that person make an impact on you?

Read

Invite someone to read aloud the following passage. Listen for new insights as you hear the verses being read, and then discuss the questions that follow.

So I tell you this, and insist on it in the Lord, that you must no longer live as the Gentiles do, in the futility of their thinking. They are darkened in their understanding and separated from the life of God because of the ignorance that is in them due to the hardening of their hearts. Having lost all sensitivity, they have given themselves over to sensuality so as to indulge in every kind of impurity, and they are full of greed.

That, however, is not the way of life you learned when you heard about Christ and were taught in him in accordance with the truth that is in Jesus. You were taught, with regard to your former way of life, to put off your old self, which is being corrupted by its deceitful desires; to be made new in the attitude of your minds; and to put on the new self, created to be like God in true righteousness and holiness.

Therefore each of you must put off falsehood and speak truthfully to your neighbor, for we are all members of one body. "In your anger do not sin" Do not let the sun go down while you are still angry, and do not give the devil a foothold. Anyone who has been stealing must steal no longer, but must work, doing something useful with their own hands, that they may have something to share with those in need.

Do not let any unwholesome talk come out of your mouths, but only what is helpful for building others up according to their needs, that it may benefit those who listen. And do not grieve the Holy Spirit of God, with whom you were sealed for the day of redemption. Get rid of all bitterness, rage and anger, brawling and slander, along with every form of malice. Be kind and compassionate to one another, forgiving each other, just as in Christ God forgave you.

EPHESIANS 4:17–32

How does Paul describe our former state before coming to Christ? What are we now required to put aside in order to follow Christ?

How do our words make or break our influence? Why do our words matter to God?

Watch

Play the video segment for session four (see the streaming video access provided on the inside front cover). As you watch, use the following outline to record any thoughts or concepts that stand out to you.

We all have influence. The question is, when it comes to fighting for racial healing, are we using our influence to be a part of the solution or a part of the problem?

If you truly want to influence the people in your neighborhood, your workplace, your school, and everywhere else, you have to carry both confidence and calmness.

Confidence means being authentic with others and not putting up a false front. We all have an edge to us. Are we willing to let the world see it? Have the confidence to be who you are.

We also need calmness when fighting for diversity. We need to have principles, but we also need to be polite. It's important to know how to de-escalate things quickly.

A few guardrails to put in place when it comes to using your influence online:

Pray before you post

Pause before you post

Host before you post

Just don't post

When we use social media wisely, it creates change. The digital age is exposing many ugly things that used to get swept under the rug. They are now in the light for everyone to see.

After you've gone through these four guardrails, if you still feel at peace, by all means post. Don't diminish your voice. You have something to say. Use your voice and say it well!

Discuss

Take a few minutes with your group members to discuss what you just watched, and then explore these concepts in Scripture.

1. What stood out to you from listening to John and Wayne today? How can you identify with the stories they shared?

2. How do you react to the idea that *you* are a person of influence? Who are some of the people in your life who look to you for guidance and instruction?

3. How can the choice to remain confident and calm affect the influence you have on others? On the flip side, how does being emotionally reactive or responding in chaos affect your influence? Can you share a few examples?

4. **Read John 18:19–40.** Jesus had every right to feel rattled and be reactive as he faced these trials before the high priest and Pilate. How does he instead model confidence and calmness as he is questioned? How is Peter's response in stark contrast?

5. Whether you use your influence in person or online, how do you stay mindful to speak the truth in love and yet not let any unwholesome talk come out of your mouth, as the apostle Paul encourages in Ephesians 4:15 and 25–29?

6. Which guardrails for posting online were most beneficial for you? How will you be sure to speak up when you're passionate about something but find wise counsel when you're in pain? What kind of further encouragement or accountability do you need from your group?

Respond

Review the outline for the video teaching and any notes you took. In the space below, write down your most significant takeaway from this session.

Pray

Pray as a group before you close your time together. Thank God for the influence he has given you, both in person and online. Ask him for the courage to be confident and calm in the way you use your influence for his glory. Pray that he will help you to be mindful of the ways you speak the truth in love and use your words of influence to build up and defend instead of tear down. Use the space below to keep track of prayer requests and group updates.

Name   Request/Praise

_____   _____

_____   _____

_____   _____

_____   _____

_____   _____

_____   _____

_____   _____

BETWEEN-SESSIONS PERSONAL STUDY

Reflect on the material you covered during this week's group time by engaging in the following personal studies. Each day offers a short reading adapted from *God and Race*, along with a few reflection questions to take you deeper into the theme of this week's study. Be sure to read the reflection questions and make a few notes in your guide about the experience. At the start of your next session, you will have a few minutes to share any insights that you learned.

Day One: Align Your Influence

Read Mark 12:28–34 and 1 Corinthians 13:1–13.

We live in a day and age where influence is quantified (and monetized) by online followers, likes, and retweets. Which is great for the people who can capitalize on it but dangerous for the rest of us. How many times have you seen something posted online that you know a person would never say in person? The truth is, we have to be just as mindful of our words online as we do in person. Words hurt just as bad in print as they do in real life.

Back in the day, crowds gathered in stadiums or coliseums to discuss social issues. But today, many of these discussions happen online in the arenas we call Twitter, Facebook, and Instagram. These arenas have a constant open-mic policy. But just because we have new arenas doesn't mean we have new rules. The Word of God is still our rulebook as Christians. It's still where we turn to learn how to interact with people—whether in person or online.

In a world full of influencers, it's easy to feel like we will never make a difference. But whether you know it or not—or believe it or not—you have influence. Even if the only person you have looking up to you is the little one under your care in your home, you have influence. If you want to work toward a diverse future of unity and reconciliation, you need to know how to use your influence in person and online, because the conversations you have with people matter. Racial healing will not come from one perfect post, but it will come in the culmination of millions of conversations, and you are responsible for some of those conversations.

Influence is more about respect than reach. So be confident in who God created you to be and the specific part you have to play regarding diversity and racial healing. And if you decide to focus on your online influence, please practice the guardrails discussed in the teaching session and in the following pages of this study guide.

1. How would you characterize your influence online and in person? Is there a difference between the two? If so, why?

2. What does it mean to say, "Influence is more about respect than reach"? How have you seen this to be true in your life?

3. How does the Greatest Commandment in Mark 12:28–34 provide the ultimate guardrail for how to use your influence? Think about the last few times you posted something online. How well would you rate on loving God and loving others in those moments?

4. According to Paul in 1 Corinthians 13:1–13, what does it look like to influence from a place of love? How will you stay mindful of wielding a loving kind of influence?

Close out your time by asking God to show you areas where you have room to influence out of a deeper place of love. Pray that you will find love as your motivation to influence, rather than influence as your motivation to love.

Day Two: Pray and Listen

Read James 1:19 and 1 Thessalonians 5:12–18.

When social media first came out, it was just a fun (and faster) way to communicate with each other. But these days, the things we have to say have real ramifications, which means we should get into the habit of sharing our posts with God in prayer before we share them with the world. Prayer not only realigns our heart and our motives toward God's heart, but it also allows us to listen to what God has to say. Learning how to listen, first to God and then to others, is the starting point for using our influence.

Your influence begins with your ears before it reaches your mouth and fingers. So, pray and listen to God before you post. If you don't feel peace about your post as you pray, take a step back and reevaluate *what* you're saying and *how* you're saying it. Ask yourself two important questions. First, *does this post promote peace?* Second, *is this post unifying?* Next, ask these questions to make sure you're listening as you go:

- Am I listening to God in prayer to learn or am I listening to respond?
- Do I care as much about God's thoughts as I care about the problem?
- Will I be content even if I don't get any credit for leading people to a solution?

These are crucial questions to consider, especially when you're learning to listen to God and others on the journey toward racial healing. Remember, your posts can lead to peace or to problems. Sometimes, the only way you'll know which outcome will occur is by listening to God in prayer and by listening to trusted others who speak into your life.

1. What do you think would happen on social media if everyone followed the advice in James 1:19? Why?

2. Take a scroll through your last few posts online and consider your last few conversations. How well did you do at being prayerful, quick to listen, slow to speak, and slow to become angry? Which area needs the most improvement in your life?

3. What advice does Paul give the Thessalonians about living at peace with one another? Which of these encouragements do you need to start practicing in your own life?

4. What specific circumstances will you commit to prayer continually in your community and on the journey toward racial healing? How can you give thanks to God for the distance you've traveled on the journey so far?

Close out your time by expressing to God your desire to listen and pray before you post or engage in conversation. Ask him to help you make this a consistent practice as a way to love him and love others in the way that you wield your influence.

Day Three: Pause and Look

Read Proverbs 10:8, 11–14, 18–21, 31–32 and 1 Peter 3:8–16.

Social media is a great tool, but it's a horrible place to vent. Venting isn't bad. It's a normal part of being human—and it's never healthy to tell people to stuff their feelings down. But when something triggers your emotions and makes you want to quickly respond, it's important to first pause and take a good look at the situation.

Quick, emotionally driven posts are a good indicator that your *pain* is driving you, not your *passion*. Social media is not the place to vent this pain you are feeling. If you need to vent, look up from your phone and find a good friend, a counselor, or another safe place, but please don't work out your painful emotions in such a public and permanent place. This encouragement is for the good of others—but it is mostly for your own good.

Whether you're posting or responding to a comment, it's good to get into the habit of hitting the *pause* button and looking up from your phone before you hit the *post* button. It's good to take a couple of deep breaths first and then ask yourself the following questions:

- Am I reacting emotionally here?
- Am I feeling pain underneath my passion?
- Is this post intended to help or to hurt?
- Does this post disciple or divide?
- Who is on the other side of this post?

Then ask yourself: *What opportunities am I missing to love or learn from someone right in front of me because I am too busy posting my opinions?* You will most likely realize this happens more often than you would like to admit! Instead, the next time you enter into a conversation—especially a conversation with someone who doesn't look like you—consciously tell yourself to *look* at them. If you're in person, pause and get your face out of your phone. If you're online, pause before you post and take a look at the rest of the person's profile. Get curious about who he or she is and what things that person likes. Choose to look and see him or her as a human rather than the recipient (or target) of your next post.

1. Who have you missed in real life lately because you've been too focused on posting on your phone? How would you benefit from pausing before you make a post?

2. Proverbs 10 has a lot to say about the way we use our mouths, our words, and our minds. What insights stand out to you from these verses you read?

3. How can pausing prevent you from the foolish and wicked ways described in the Proverbs passage? How does looking at someone and truly seeing him or her as another human—as a fellow image-bearer of God—change the way you respond?

4. What encouragement does Peter give on how to live a good life? How do the habits of pausing before posting and looking people in the eye contribute to a good life?

Close out your time by asking God to help you pause and look before you post. Ask that you will begin to take greater notice and offer more care and concern for the way your words and your presence affects the people around you—both in person and online.

Day Four: Host and Learn

Read Deuteronomy 5:1–22 and Philippians 4:1–9.

When it comes to expressing your opinions about racial issues online, it's important to first consider whether you would be willing to have the conversation that you are about to start *in person*. If you are willing to host an in-person conversation with someone who has a different point of view—and not just hiding behind your keyboard—there is a next step to take. *Call a friend of a different color and a different perspective than you and ask for that person's thoughts.* Listen to that person and seek to learn something from him or her.

Don't be like all those "keyboard warriors" out there who are only interested in hearing themselves speak (or type). Their influence gets lost the moment they choose to post their passionate— often painful—opinions online rather than connect with someone in real life. Without human connection and conversation, we lose perspective. Because we are creatures of habit, the less connection and conversation we have, the more we get stuck and stop learning. So, sometimes God will break us out of our regularly scheduled programming to teach us something. It's the only way we're willing to listen and learn.

Hosting a conversation before you post will help you avoid pitfalls of misinformation, misunderstandings, and sharing your well-meaning thoughts with a lack of love. It is the best way to learn from others, because firsthand experiences—especially when talking about issues of race—are so valuable. Of course, this takes more time, but it's worth it. The results may not be *immediate*, but if you persevere, you will find that the payoff is *immense*.

1. The Bible is filled with stories of times when people gathered to have important discussions and learn crucial lessons. What kind of gathering happens in Deuteronomy 5:1–22? How is this gathering significant for God's people?

2. Paul sends what could be considered a modern-day "post" in his letter to the Philippians. How does Paul advise the church to approach every situation? How would your interactions online change if you read this passage before every post?

3. How does practicing the peace of God go hand in hand with learning from others?

4. How will you make peace a practice and a priority in your life when it comes to posting and the way you engage in real conversations on racial equity and healing?

Close out your time by asking God to reveal the opportunities he has given you to host real conversations and learn from others. Pray that you will find his peace and healing as you engage in real-life conversations with those who have a different perspective than you.

Day Five: Don't Post but Still Influence

Read 2 Kings 5:1–14; 1 Corinthians 10:23–24; and Matthew 9:35–38.

Your voice matters. But the sobering truth is that the world will get on just fine without your opinion. So when in doubt about whether or not to post, it's okay to say no and put down the phone. You don't have to post even if you're passionate about something. You can pick your battles wisely and keep those battles in person if you don't have peace about posting.

Besides, how many times have you said something you wished you could take back? Sometimes, in the heat of the moment, you've certainly said things you don't mean and hurt people you love in the process. If there's anything to learn from such moments of regret, it's that history belongs to the humble. Prideful, powerful people make history books, but those who lay down their lives for others, metaphorically and literally, are remembered forever.

Social media is a great tool and a necessary ally as we move toward racial healing. When used correctly, it can bear a ton of excellent fruit. But when used painfully, it can bring a ton of destruction in the name of racism, off-colored jokes, generational bias, and political idolatry. We are living in a historic moment, and people will read about these times. When they do, what type of story will it be? Will it be a story reinforced by your last heated or hurtful social media post? Or will it be a story about millions of people who decided to create change by having conversations and influencing the people right in front of them?

Let's hope it will be a story of how we got out of our comfort zones and looked beyond ourselves to reverse the plight of racism and grant full privileges to *all* humans. We are all influencers, and we all have a part to play as history unfolds. So let's play it well.

1. The story we read in 2 Kings 5 is about a man with privilege, power, and a problem. Yet the true heroes of the story are a captive girl from Israel, an anonymous messenger, and other unknown servants—all of whom are able to influence Naaman's actions. What does this tell you about who God uses to be people of influence in the world?

2. We all can be influencers, but if we want to be influencers for the kingdom of God, we need to understand what it means to steward our influence well. What does Paul say to the Corinthians in this regard? How do his words inspire you?

3. Think about some of the words you might have posted recently. Do you have any posts and comments that you need to delete or profiles that you need to change?

4. Choosing not to post isn't about erasing evidence but about cultivating compassion and changing the way you talk about people moving forward. What does compassion mean to you? How does the compassion of Jesus change lives in Matthew 9:35–38?

Close out your time by talking to God about the people who are watching and listening to you. Ask that he would continue to help you be a healthy influencer for his kingdom.

For Next Week

Use the space below to write any insights or questions that you want to discuss at the next group meeting. Before your next session, read chapters 12–14 in *God and Race*.

A HOUSE THAT LOOKS LIKE HEAVEN

And what does the Lord require of you
but to do justice, and to love kindness,
and to walk humbly with your God?
Micah 6:8 ESV

Welcome

During the course of this study, we have discussed how having helpful conversations about race requires us to move beyond black fists and white knuckles and to have *open hands*. We've looked at how this journey starts in our *hearts*. We've talked about allowing God to search our hearts and how we respond to issues such as *privilege* and *profiling*. We've discussed who we are *inviting into our homes* and how we can make diversity an intentional part of our lives. In the last session, we looked at how we are *using our influence* when it comes to conversations on race.

But we can't stop there. When it comes to racism—a spiritual problem in need of a spiritual solution—we have to take an honest look at how our *churches* are contributing to the solution. Are they committing to be places of diversity and unity? Or are they perpetuating the very same problems we're trying to combat? At the end of the day, God's plan for the world is his church.

So, how are we doing in executing that plan?

The most popular picture of the church in the Bible is that of a house. So, it's safe to say that as people who make up the church, we belong to the "house of God" or the "house of heaven." But just like the trap we can fall into in our homes where everyone looks, thinks, acts, and even *dresses* the same, we can fall into the same trap in our churches. This is why reading about the early church in the New Testament is so vital to understanding the vision God has for his house. They were a diverse group unified by their common belief in Jesus as the Messiah.

Sadly, somewhere along the way we have forgotten this vision. Yet there is still hope for the church to be the house that looks like heaven—the house that best represents God. There is still hope for the church to lead the way in bringing racial healing to the world because of the part we all have to play. But we have to first take a hard look at the house of God and admit the truth about where we are today. After all, we can't get to where we want to be until we know where we are right now. This is how we determine where we go from here.

Consider

Begin your final group time by inviting those in the group to share their insights from last week's personal study. Then, to kick things off, discuss one of the following questions:

- How do you respond to the idea that God's plan for the world is his church?

— *or* —

- How would you assess the way the church as a whole is doing when it comes to committing to be places of unity and diversity?

Read

Invite someone to read aloud the following passage. Listen for new insights as you hear the verses being read, and then discuss the questions that follow.

You, my brothers and sisters, were called to be free. But do not use your freedom to indulge the flesh; rather, serve one another humbly in love. For the entire law is fulfilled in keeping this one command: "Love your neighbor as yourself." If you bite and devour each other, watch out or you will be destroyed by each other.

So I say, walk by the Spirit, and you will not gratify the desires of the flesh. For the flesh desires what is contrary to the Spirit, and the Spirit what is contrary to the flesh. They are in conflict with each other, so that you are not to do whatever you want. But if you are led by the Spirit, you are not under the law.

The acts of the flesh are obvious: sexual immorality, impurity and debauchery; idolatry and witchcraft; hatred, discord, jealousy, fits of rage, selfish ambition, dissensions, factions and envy; drunkenness, orgies, and the like. I warn you, as I did before, that those who live like this will not inherit the kingdom of God.

But the fruit of the Spirit is love, joy, peace, forbearance, kindness, goodness, faithfulness, gentleness and self-control. Against such things there is no law. Those who belong to Christ Jesus have crucified the flesh with its passions and desires. Since we live by the Spirit, let us keep in step with the Spirit. Let us not become conceited, provoking and envying each other.

GALATIANS 5:13–26

What are some of the ways that Paul says believers should act toward one another?

What does it mean to walk by the Spirit? What happens when believers do this?

Watch

Play the video segment for session five (see the streaming video access provided on the inside front cover). As you watch, use the following outline to record any thoughts or concepts that stand out to you.

As we've discussed, Revelation 7:9 paints a picture of where the church is headed—a diverse multitude of people from every tribe and nation gathered before God's throne.

Acts 2 tells us how the church started. The believers were *unified* together and surrounded by a *diverse* group of people—and that is the moment God decided to launch the church.

We are in between those two points with a whole lot of work to do. So, how can each of us help to make our churches become houses that look more like heaven? *We take inventory and admit the truth.* If you are a church leader, here are three good questions to ask:

What are the racial demographics of your church? Are they similar or different from the demographics of your city? Does your church reflect the diversity of your city?

What message is your church communicating to the world? What is your brand?

Do you have diversity in your church leadership?

But this session isn't just for church leaders. It's for anyone who is a part of the church in any capacity. So, we have to ask three tough questions about ourselves:

Am I willing to stay and be a part of a diverse church even when it's difficult?

How can I help my church become more diverse?

Is church actually the most diverse hour of my week?

Where do we go from here?

Act justly

Love kindness

Walk humbly

Discuss

Take a few minutes with your group members to discuss what you just watched, and then explore these concepts in Scripture.

1. What stood out to you from listening to John and Wayne today? How can you identify with the stories they shared?

2. Of all the questions asked by John and Wayne—to both church leaders and laypeople—which struck a deep chord with you? Why?

3. In Acts 2:41–47, we are given a glimpse into the early church and a vision for our churches today. As you read this passage, what stands out to you about this small group of early Christians? How does this inspire you to make a difference in your church?

4. The commands to *act justly, love kindness,* and *walk humbly* come from a moment of God's righteous anger. What is the context of Micah 6:8? Why is this important for us to understand in the way we read and interpret this passage today?

5. **Read Ephesians 1:15–23.** What gifts *from* God allow us to walk humbly *with* God? Why is Paul giving thanks for the Ephesians? In what ways can you give thanks to God for where your church is and yet still continue to pray for it to grow?

6. What specific steps can your church take to become more of "a house that looks like heaven" as it makes diversity more of a priority? How will you be a part of taking action in these particular areas on the journey toward racial healing?

Respond

Review the outline for the video teaching and any notes you took. In the space below, write down your most significant takeaway from this session.

Pray

Close this study by praying as a group. Thank God for the description he gave us of the early church in Acts and the vision he gave us for where the church is headed in Revelation. Ask God for the wisdom to act justly, love kindness, and walk humbly as we open our hands, open our hearts, open our homes, and open our houses of God for the sake of racial unity and healing. Use the space below to keep track of any final prayer requests and group updates.

Name   Request/Praise

_____   _____

_____   _____

_____   _____

_____   _____

_____   _____

_____   _____

_____   _____

FINAL PERSONAL STUDY

Reflect on the material you covered during this week's group time by engaging in the following personal studies. Each day offers a short reading adapted from *God and Race*, along with a few reflection questions to take you deeper into the theme of this week's study. Be sure to read the reflection questions and make a few notes in your guide about the experience. In the coming days, share any insights that you learned with one of your fellow group members.

Day One: Back to the Blueprint

Read Revelation 7:9–12; Matthew 5:13–16; and John 8:12–20.

The end of the human story is every tribe, tongue, and nation unified together before God. But we certainly aren't there yet. Ask any non-believers about their perceptions of the church, and odds are they will talk about the division in the church before they talk about diversity. Somewhere along the way, we took our eyes off the blueprint. We lost sight of what it looks like to *be* the church and *build* the church in the way Jesus instructed. Jesus is the master-builder of the church, but it's as though we've taken construction into our own hands these days. And in doing so, we've drifted far from the original plans.

Regardless of whether or not you work for a church, if you consider yourself a follower of Jesus, then you have a part to play in the church—and not just in your local church but in the global church. Getting back to the blueprint of what Jesus intended for the church as the "house of heaven" means having open-handed conversations about God and race in your heart, in your home, in your community, and in your church. It also means using your voice for good wherever you go as you represent the church during these intense and polarizing times.

The house of God as the church of God *can*, and *should*, lead the way in bringing racial healing to the world. And you have a part to play in getting back to Jesus' blueprint—the blueprint that says we are to be "salt of the earth," "the light of the world," and a "city on a hill." We are God's plan for the world, so let's step up and do what God created us to do. Let's get back to becoming a *diverse* and *unified* house that looks like heaven.

1. When was the last time you used a blueprint to build something? How does this idea of the church being God's blueprint resonate with you? What does it stir in you?

2. When we look at the picture given to us in Revelation 7:9 of a "great multitude that no one could count," we see there is more to the story in verses 11–12. Who else is with the great multitude of people? Why is this significant?

3. Which description of followers of Christ stands out to you from Matthew 5:13–16: "salt of the earth," "light of the world," or "town built on a hill"? Why? How does that metaphor inspire you as you step up to play a role in the journey toward racial healing?

4. We have the opportunity to be the light of the world because of Jesus. Under what authority does Jesus claim to be the light of the world in John 8:12–20? What does Jesus' authority mean for you as you seek to follow his blueprint?

Close your time by asking God to show you a picture of how you can follow the blueprint he set for the church through Jesus. Pray that the church will find its way back to the blueprint and that you will gain fresh vision for the diverse and unifying power of God and the church.

Day Two: Diverse by Design

Read Galatians 3:26–29 and Acts 2:1–21.

Segregation didn't happen in the church by accident. It *happened by design*. In 1792, two black men, Richard Allen and Absalom Jones, walked into a church to sit and pray. What these men didn't realize was that they had sat in seats reserved for white people, and they were soon forcibly pulled out of those seats. Allen went on to establish the first historically black Christian denomination, the African Methodist Episcopal Denomination. In other words, *the black church started because of racism in the white church.*

You would think the church would have led the way in bringing about racial healing. But historically, instead of leading, the church has lagged behind. Instead of stomping out racism, it has tended to put a stamp of approval on things associated with it. But people are starting to wake up, and the tide is starting to turn. Thousands have decided to finally stand and say what the white congregants watching Allen and Jones should have said back in 1792: "that's enough." Many are starting to say that church must again be a place where there is "neither Jew nor Gentile" but where all are "one in Christ Jesus" (Galatians 3:28).

What was once segregated by design can actually become diverse by design. We just need to go back to the blueprint that Jesus established for the church. Seven weeks after the death and resurrection of Jesus, his followers gathered. And while they had no idea what to *do*, they had clear instructions on how to *be*. So they started where they were—all with one accord in one place, together in *unity*. As a very diverse group of people, these early believers most likely had more questions than answers, but they knew they needed to be *together*. They were *diverse by design*, and we can be too as part of the church today.

1. How do you respond to the story of Richard Allen and Absalom Jones? Has your church experience been one of diversity or of division?

2. Why do you think the church has lagged in bringing about racial healing? What crucial step could your church take to change the tide of racial unity in your community?

3. What would it take for the church of today to look like the church described in Galatians 3:26–29? How would this old vision of the church make things new for you and for others in your community?

4. What part can you play in helping the church get back to being diverse by design like the church in Acts 2? How do your talents and skills match up with the needs of your church as you journey toward open hands and open hearts regarding God and race?

Close out your time by asking God to give you a greater vision for how the church can get back to being diverse by design. Pray for a spirit of humility as you offer your skills and talents in the places where your local church has the greatest needs.

Day Three: An Honest Assessment

Read Matthew 12:30–37; Mark 11:15–18; and John 4:1–26.

Inviting diversity into the church is a long and difficult process. But we have to start somewhere . . . so why not start with an honest assessment of where we are? Guilt is not the goal in this conversation, and there's no place for shame. However, over the years, many church congregants and leaders have realized that in order to move forward toward rebuilding a diverse church, we first have to be honest about the reality of the church. The most helpful place to start being honest is by asking questions—questions like the ones you heard in the teaching this week. Questions about your church such as:

- Does your church reflect the diversity of your city or your area?
- Does your church communicate a safe and welcoming message for ALL?
- Does your church leadership reflect the diversity of the community?
- Are you willing to stay at your church rather than go elsewhere?
- Are you willing to be a part of the solution rather than the problem?
- Are you mindful of bringing diversity into other areas of your life?

Your honest answers to these questions will give you an honest assessment of your church and the part you have to play in it, in your community, and in your home. Remember, the goal of this assessment is not guilt or shame; it's to locate the center of reality. It's to seek progress over perfection. And it's to actually *be diverse*, not just present a *picture of diversity*.

It's time for the church to be more mindful of the message we are sending the world. We need to recognize diversity starts from the top, not from the bottom, and that diversity is essential in practice, not just theory. So, if you're going to ask your church to make diversity a priority in their relationships, in their messaging, and in their leadership, make sure you are doing the same. Stop looking the other way and waiting for someone else to take this honest assessment. Now is the time for you to step up and lead or assist in this charge.

1. How would you answer the first set of questions from today's session regarding your church?

2. How would you answer the second set of questions from today's session regarding yourself and your posture toward diversity in your church?

3. In what ways did Jesus model this idea of taking an honest assessment of a current situation in the stories found in Matthew 12:30–37 and Mark 11:15–18?

4. If Jesus were talking with you over a cup of coffee like he was talking to the Samaritan woman over a jar of water at the well (see John 4), what would he call out in you? What situation would he accurately assess or correct for you?

Close out your time today by talking with God about the honest assessment you've taken of where you are in your life and in your church. Ask God to give you comfort in seeing the truth of where you are and encouragement for moving forward toward diversity and restoration.

Day Four: From Passivity to Activity

Read John 4:27–42 and Mark 2:13–17.

When the white church closed its fist and held on to deeply rooted beliefs that they were superior, thousands of congregants stayed silent—even when they knew something was wrong. Segregation is the fruit of passivism. And racism is what happened when the white community bowed at the altar of comfort continually over time. But *we have the opportunity to work toward diversity and clear our hands of anything that resembles hierarchy based on the color of our skin.* We are one body of believers united under something much more significant than our sin—we are united by the cross of Jesus Christ. And when one part of the body is hurting, we are all hurting. This means that when you see people treating someone unjustly for the color of their skin, it's your responsibility to stand up and take action by saying, "that's enough."

If the honest assessment you took of yourself and your church revealed that you have farther to go than you thought, don't lose heart. It's easier to move from passivity to activity when you're armed with the truth. So, just take a deep breath and start with one small step toward the necessary action. You don't have to change everything overnight. Just begin with the need or the group of people God has placed directly in front of you. You may not be where you want to be, and the church you're a part of may have a long battle ahead of it. But connecting with the next person you meet who doesn't look like you is a perfect place to start building diversity and working toward racial healing.

The only way to clear your hands of the sins of the past and let go of any old system of oppression you've held onto is to open your hands and open your hearts to what God is trying to show you. So let the old ways fall to the floor and get ready to receive what God has next for you. As you do, you will move beyond black fists and white knuckles to take action.

1. How has segregation been the fruit of passivism? What altars have kept people from taking action against segregation (altars such as comfort, approval, and other things we aren't willing to give up for the sake of fighting against racism)?

2. In what ways do you sense God asking you or telling you to move from passivity to activity in the fight for racial justice and healing?

3. Read the rest of the story of Jesus and the Samaritan woman at the well told in John 4:27–42. How did the woman go from passivity to activity when Jesus revealed the truth of her situation? What was the ripple effect of her activity?

4. Faith in Jesus prompted Levi (Matthew) to turn away from his old life as a tax collector and follow after Christ. What is Jesus calling you to put aside as you follow him?

Close your time by speaking with God about the sin of your passivity and the truth of your activity. Ask him to give you the strength to press through the difficulty of acknowledging your role in the sins of the past as you commit to being a part of his movement in the present.

Day Five: Finding Your Voice

Read Luke 10:25–37 and 1 Peter 2:1–17.

As Jesus followers, we are children of God and citizens of heaven. This is our identity. However, there is a rising number of Christians today who identify with their political party before their identity in God. "Out of order" may seem like an odd phrase, but we all intuitively understand that when something is out of order, the entire system has the potential to break down. The same is true for us. God created us in his image, and we function best when we function according to his design. But when we get our priorities out of order, things fall apart.

We're on a journey toward unity and diversity, but we've found ourselves on a detour—a detour that looks like many of us getting caught up in our political parties rather than our identities as citizens of heaven. Somehow, we've traded polarizing political opinions for unity in God. And this has significant racial implications when we either don't find our voice on the journey toward racial justice or we use it in misdirected ways. Finding our prophetic voice means finding the ability to speak God's word into a situation.

We can get so caught up in trying to have a political voice that we lose our prophetic one. But if the house of God is going to lead the way into the future of racial diversity, healing, and reconciliation, we need to recapture our prophetic voice as individuals and as a united body of believers. Spiritual leaders are those who have spearheaded the most significant movements in the history of the world. And when the church is at its best, it can change the world. So let's be the change we wish to see by finding our prophetic voice.

1. How has the church been split by political polarization? In what ways have you felt this in your personal life?

2. What comes to mind when you think of the word *prophetic*? How has this session redefined your idea or interpretation of what it means to have a prophetic voice?

3. Centuries ago, owners of enslaved people heard about Jesus' call to love and the fruits of the Spirit, and then went home and forced their neighbors into lives of slavery. How does this example inform the importance of finding your prophetic voice?

4. How does the example of the Great Commandment wrapped up in the parable of the Good Samaritan in Luke 10:25–37 inform the way you use your voice today—both inside and outside the church?

Close out your time by speaking to God about the political polarization happening around you and the prophetic voice that he has given you. Ask him to help you set straight any priorities that have gotten out of order as you seek to follow after Christ.

CLOSING WORDS

Thank you for joining us for this *God and Race* study. It has been a joy to walk alongside you on your quest for open-handed conversations on faith and race.

Remember that no matter how diverse and polarized things may seem in the present, we know the end of the story. The end of the story is a beautiful picture of a diverse group of people worshiping unified together before God. Let that fill you with hope today.

When people encountered Jesus, they were challenged and changed. Some went away angry. Some went away sad. But no one left feeling indifferent. And that's our hope for each one of you. The rocks of racism are real, and they aren't easy to shake off. And fighting for unity and diversity in the church is not easy. But the people who make history and bring about reconciliation are those who don't let the poison of racism and passivism paralyze them.

We are the image bearers of the divine and agents of reconciliation here to make a difference in the world. We want to be remembered as the era of the church that built bridges instead of barriers and brought a polarized country together at the foot of the cross. So it's time to face the hurt the church has caused over racism and let the healing process begin. We are called by God to be agents of that healing.

The road to racial healing is a long, winding path full of detours and roadblocks. And it feels like a tiring, uphill journey most of the way. So here's our benediction for you:

May you find comfort and encouragement in Paul's words to the Galatians: "Let us not become weary in doing good, for at the proper time we will reap a harvest if we do not give up" (6:9). May you continue to build a house of God that looks like the house of heaven—with open hands, open minds, open hearts, and church doors that swing wide.

Peace and grace,

— Wayne and John

LEADER'S GUIDE

Thank you for your willingness to lead your group through this study. What you have chosen to do is valuable and will make a great difference in the lives of others. The rewards of being a leader are different from those of participating, and we hope that as you lead you will find your own walk with Jesus deepened by the experience.

God and Race is a five-session study built around video content and small-group interaction. As a group leader, think of yourself as the host. Your job is to take care of your guests by managing the behind-the-scenes details so that when everyone arrives, they can enjoy their time together. Your role as the leader is not to answer all the questions or reteach the content—the video, book, and study guide will do that work. Your job is to guide the experience and cultivate your small group into a kind of teaching community. This will make it a place for members to process, question, and reflect—not receive more instruction.

There are several elements in this leader's guide that will help you as you structure your study and reflection time, so be sure to follow along and take advantage of each one.

Starting the Group Time

Before your first meeting, make sure the group members have a copy of this study guide. Alternately, you can hand out the study guides at your first meeting and give the group members some time to look over the material and ask any preliminary questions. Also make sure they are aware that they have access to the videos at any time through the streaming code provided on the inside front cover. At your first meeting, distribute a sheet of paper around the room and have the members write down their name, phone number, and email address so you can keep in touch with them during the week.

Generally, the ideal size for a group is eight to ten people, which will ensure that everyone has enough time to participate in discussions. If you have more people, you might want to break up the main group into smaller subgroups. Encourage those who show up at the first meeting to commit to attending the duration of the study, as this will help the group members get to know one another, create stability for the group, and help you as the leader to know how to best prepare each week.

Each of the sessions begins with an opening reflection. The questions that follow in the "Consider" section serve as an ice-breaker to get the group members thinking about the general topic at hand. Some people may want to tell a long story in response to one of these questions, but the goal is to keep the answers brief. Ideally, you want everyone in the group to get a chance to answer, so try to keep the responses to a minute or less. If you have talkative group members, say up front that everyone needs to limit their answer to one minute.

Give the group members a chance to answer, but tell them to feel free to pass if they wish. With the rest of the study, it's generally not a good idea to have everyone answer every question—a free-flowing discussion is more desirable. But with the opening icebreaker-type questions, you can go around the circle. Encourage shy people to share, but don't force them.

At your first meeting, let the group members know each session contains a personal study section that they can use to reflect more on the content during the week. While this is an optional exercise, it will help the members cement the concepts presented during the group study time and encourage them to spend time each day in God's Word. Invite them to bring to the next meeting any questions and insights they uncovered while reading, especially if they had a breakthrough moment or didn't understand something.

Weekly Preparation

As the leader, there are a few things you should do to prepare for each meeting:

- *Read through the session.* This will help you to become more familiar with the content and know how to structure the discussion times.
- *Decide how the videos will be used.* Determine whether you want the members to watch the videos (via the streaming access code found on the inside front cover) or together as a group.
- *Decide which questions you want to discuss.* Based on the amount and length of group discussion, you may not be able to get through all the questions, so choose four to five that you definitely want to cover.

- Be *familiar with the questions you want to discuss*. When the group meets, you'll be watching the clock, so you want to make sure you are familiar with the questions you have selected. In this way, you'll ensure you have the material more deeply in your mind than your group members.
- *Pray for your group*. Pray for your group members throughout the week and ask God to lead them as they study his Word.

In many cases, there will be no one "right" answer to the question. Answers will vary, especially when the group members are being asked to share their personal experiences.

Structuring the Discussion Time

You will need to determine with your group how long you want to meet each week so you can plan your time accordingly. Generally, most groups like to meet for sixty minutes to two hours, so you could use one of the following schedules:

As the group leader, it is up to you to keep track of the time and keep things on schedule. You might want to set a timer for each segment so both you and the group members know when your time is up. (There are some good phone apps for timers that play a gentle chime or other pleasant sound instead of a disruptive noise.)

Don't be concerned if the group members are quiet or slow to share. People are often quiet when they are pulling together their ideas, and this might be a new experience for them. Just ask a question and let it hang in the air until someone shares. You can then say, "Thank you. What about others? What came to you when you watched that portion of the teaching?"

SECTION	60 min	90 min	120 min
Welcome (members arrive)	5 min	5 min	10 min
Consider & Read (discuss the opening questions)	10 min	15 min	15 min
Watch (watch the video teaching)	15 min	15 min	15 min
Discuss (discuss the group questions)	25 min	40 min	60 min
Respond & Pray (close the group time)	5 min	15 min	20 min

Group Dynamics

Leading a group through *God and Race* will prove to be highly rewarding both to you and your group members. But you still may encounter challenges along the way! Discussions can get off track. Group members may not be sensitive to the needs and ideas of others. Some might worry they will be expected to talk about matters that make them feel awkward. Others may express comments that result in disagreements. To help ease this strain on you and the group, consider the following ground rules:

- When someone raises a question or comment that is off the main topic, suggest that you deal with it another time, or, if you feel led to go in that direction, let the group know you will be spending some time discussing it.

- If someone asks a question that you don't know how to answer, admit it and move on. At your discretion, feel free to invite group members to comment on questions that call for personal experience.
- If you find one or two people are dominating the discussion time, direct a few questions to others in the group. Outside the main group time, ask the more dominating members to help you draw out the quieter ones. Work to make them a part of the solution instead of part of the problem.
- When a disagreement occurs, encourage the group members to process the matter in love. Encourage those on opposite sides to restate what they heard the other side say about the matter, and then invite each side to evaluate if that perception is accurate. Lead the group in examining other Scriptures related to the topic and look for common ground.

When any of these issues arise, encourage your group members to follow these words from the Bible: "Love one another" (John 13:34), "If it is possible, as far as it depends on you, live at peace with everyone" (Romans 12:18), "Whatever is true . . . noble . . . right . . . if anything is excellent or praiseworthy—think about such things" (Philippians 4:8), and "Be quick to listen, slow to speak and slow to become angry" (James 1:19). This will make your group time more rewarding and beneficial for everyone who attends.

Thank you again for your willingness to lead your group. May God reward your efforts and dedication, equip you to guide your group in the weeks ahead, and make your time together in *God and Race* fruitful as you engage in these discussions on race in your church.

God and Race is available wherever books are sold.

For more information about the authors and the book,
please go to godandrace.com.

We Can Choose to Face Our Past or Be Forced to Face It

Two-time GRAMMY-winning hip-hop artist and bestselling author Lecrae inspires millions with his redemptive and gut-honest art. But when his personal life spun into chaos, he was forced to face the buried impact of unhealed wounds from his past. Along the way to restoration, he learned simple practices for lasting health and realized that the pain we all carry has the potential to be a guide to freedom for ourselves and others.

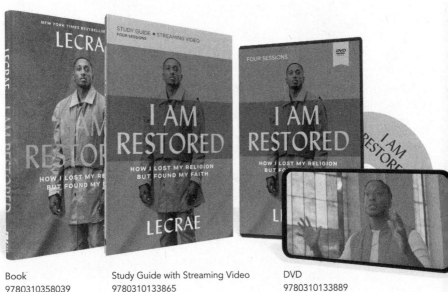

Book
9780310358039

Study Guide with Streaming Video
9780310133865

DVD
9780310133889

Available now at your favorite bookstore, or streaming video on StudyGateway.com.

There Can Be No Justice without Truth

Jemar Tisby provides a unique survey of American Christianity's racial past, revealing the ways people of faith have worked against racial justice, as well as the complicit silence of racial moderates. This 11-session video study provides a diagnosis for a racially divided American church and suggests ways to foster a more equitable and inclusive environment among God's people. Please note that some video sessions contain graphic content that viewers may find disturbing. It may not be suitable for all audiences.

Book
9780310597261

Study Guide
9780310114833

DVD
9780310102205

Available now at your favorite bookstore, or streaming video on StudyGateway.com.

Learn to Take a Stand
for Justice Today

This 10-session video study provides groups and individuals with an array of actionable items to help confront racism in relationships and in everyday life. Jemar Tisby presents a simple framework—the ARC of Racial Justice—that helps you interrogate your actions and maintain a consistent posture of antiracist action.

Tisby roots the ultimate solution in the Christian principles of love, justice, and the image of God. He issues a compelling call to dismantle a social hierarchy long stratified by skin color and provides specific, practical steps that enable you to be part of the solution to today's racial problems.

Book	Study Guide	DVD
9780310104773	9780310113225	9780310113249

Available now at your favorite bookstore,
or streaming video on MasterLectures.ZondervanAcademic.com.

Jesus Walked Away from Toxic People, and You Should Too

In this book and six-session video Bible study, bestselling author Gary Thomas draws on Jesus' example to show how the best course of action for us to take with toxic relationships is to walk away...or let the other person walk away. In the Gospels, when Jesus spoke a hard truth, sometimes the other person walked away or asked Jesus to leave—and he complied. Other times, people begged Jesus to stay, but he walked away so he could remain completely focused on the mission God had for him. We can, and should, do the same.

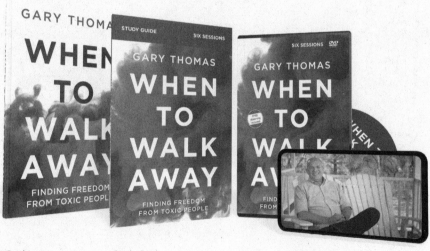

Book
9780310346760

Study Guide
9780310110248

DVD with FREE streaming
9780310110361

Available now at your favorite bookstore,
or streaming video on StudyGateway.com.

We hope you enjoyed this Bible study from John and Wayne.
Here are some other Bible studies we think you'll like.

Louie Giglio

Max Lucado

Andy Stanley

*Don't Give the Enemy
a Seat at Your Table*
Study Guide
+ Streaming Video

*You Were Made
For This Moment*
Study Guide
+ Streaming Video

*Better Decisions
Fewer Regrets*
Study Guide

—————— OUR MISSION ——————

Equipping people to understand the Scriptures, cultivate spiritual growth,
and live an inspired faith with Bible study and video resources
from today's most trusted voices.

Find your next Bible study, video series, or ministry training at:
HarperChristianResources.com

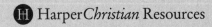